Praise for
D. Bannon

The Elements of Subtitles

"Language is a hard thing to show through text alone, especially when you have dialogue and nothing else. *The Elements of Subtitles* discusses translating and subtitling modern media and explains that subtitles need to be more than literal translations, and need to truly grasp the nature of the subject. *The Elements of Subtitles* is a must for anyone who wants to get into the world of translation or simply gain an understanding of why things are done the way they are with foreign media. Practical, user-friendly, and replete with illustrative examples, *The Elements of Subtitles* will prove to be of immense and practical value for anyone engaged in translating written expressions from other languages into English."

—Midwest Book Review

I Really, Really Like You

"We can really feel the attempt at conveying some sense of language and cultural nuance in a natural American English idiom. Translation & Subtitles: 9 out of 9."

—DVDBeaver

"At no time did the subtitles pull me out of the moment or wreck the atmosphere of the show."

—DVDTalk

The Great Queen Seondeok

"Clearly and expertly translated with English subtitling including all idioms and colloquialisms to English equivalents."

—KoreanDramas.TV

"Very clear and excellent-quality English subtitling which is not only easy and quick to read but also includes colloquial idioms."

—ForeignFilms.com

Time Between Dog & Wolf

"Translation & Subtitles: 9 out of 9."

—DVDBeaver

The Elements of Subtitles

Revised and Expanded Edition

The Elements of Subtitles

A Practical Guide to the Art of Dialogue,
Character, Context, Tone and Style
in Subtitling

Revised and Expanded Edition

D. Bannon

The Elements of Subtitles, Revised and Expanded Edition: A Practical Guide to the Art of Dialogue, Character, Context, Tone and Style in Subtitling

Foreword to the first edition © 2009 by Troy Hasbrouck
Foreword to the revised and expanded edition © 2010 by Tom Larsen

East of Eden (Eden ui dongjjok). MBC (2008-2009). Directed by So Weon-yeong. Screenplay by Na Yeon-suk & Lee Hong-ku. Translation © MBC America. Episodes 33-56 translated by D. Bannon. Reprinted with permission.
The Great Queen Seondeok (Seondeok yeowang). MBC (2009). Directed by Pak Hong-kyun & Kim Geun-hong. Screenplay by Kim Yeong-hyun & Pak Sang-yeon. Translation © MBC America. Series translated by D. Bannon. Reprinted with permission.
My Wife is a Superwoman (aka *Queen of Housewives; Naejo ui yeowang*). MBC (2009). Directed by Go Dong-sun. Screenplay by Park Ji-eun. Translation © MBC America. Series translated by D. Bannon. Reprinted with permission.
I Really, Really Like You (Jinjja jinjja joahae). MBC (2006). Directed by Kim Jin-man. Screenplay by Bae Yu-mi. Translation © YA Entertainment, LLC. Series translated by D. Bannon. Reprinted with permission.
Excerpts from *The I Really, Really Like You Reference Guide* by D. Bannon. © 2008 YA Entertainment, LLC. Reprinted with permission.
Time Between Dog & Wolf (Kye wa nukdae ui sigan; L'heure entre chien et loup). MBC (2007). Directed by Kim Jin-min. Screenplay by Han Ji-hun & Yu Yeong-jae. Translation © YA Entertainment, LLC. Series translated by D. Bannon. Reprinted with permission.

Portions of chapter 6 were published in "Subtitling: The Role of Trans-modal Translation in Global Cinema," *Translation Journal* Vol. 14 No. 2 (2010); © 2010 D. Bannon.

Originally published in 2009 in a different format.

First Revised and Expanded Edition, 2010

ISBN 978-0-557-35559-4

Every effort has been made to trace and acknowledge sources. If any credit or right has been omitted the publisher offers apologies and will rectify this in subsequent editions following notification.

For Elaine and Jessica

And I love you
as I love the dance that brings you
out of the multitude
in which you come and go.
Love changes, and in change is true.

Wendell Berry

In work of love, the body
forgets its weight. And once
again with love and singing
in my mind, I come to what
must come to me, carried
as a dancer by a song.
This grace is gravity.

Wendell Berry

Acknowledgements

A book is rarely equal to the help one received while writing it. I'm grateful to those who generously gave their time and insights. You know you who you are. I want everyone else to.

Thanks to my translation colleagues: Tom Larsen with YA Entertainment; Nahee Kim, Seong-Han Chung and Tammie Kim with MBC America; Vania Haam, Jisu Kim, Rachel Park and Steven Bammel with the American Translators Association (ATA). Thanks to Robin Conover and Troy Hasbrouck for sharing their strongly-held opinions on character and dialogue in film. Thanks to Van Warner and David Wheeler. Special thanks to my wife and daughter.

The cinema is undoubtedly
the most international of all arts.

Sergei Eisenstein

Global cinema is
the translator's cinema.

Abé Mark Nornes

Subtitles offer a way into
worlds outside of ourselves.

Atom Egoyan and Ian Balfour

Contents

From Good to Great

This may sound familiar. An amazing program from a distant land makes its way to your local theater or into your home. It's a masterpiece with a big budget, a notable screenwriter, a renowned director, a top cast, and an assortment of special effects. You have high expectations.

The program starts.

English subtitles appear.

And something goes wrong.

You notice that the English just isn't right somehow. The words are awkward. The tone is off; the flow bumpy; the style stiff. Some subtitles appear and disappear in a flash. Others stay on the screen for 30 seconds while the main character in the scene talks and talks and talks. What you were hoping would be a world-class entertainment has turned into an episode of frustration, all because of inadequate or downright horrible English subtitles.

I'm a huge fan of foreign films and TV shows, especially from Korea and Japan. For years I have been distributing Korean TV shows and movies with English subtitles in the United States. My company, YA Entertainment, has over 1,500 hours of Korean programming in its catalog—every minute of it subtitled in English. My team and I take English subtitle quality very seriously.

D. Bannon's new book, *The Elements of Subtitles,* is required reading for my internal subtitle staff. And whenever I need some temporary assistance from outside freelance subtitlers, I always ask them to read Bannon's book first. Only then can I be assured that the freelancer and I "are on the same page".

Bannon's book is the definitive guide for all working subtitle translators or for anyone who is looking to begin a career in the subtitle translation field.

We need more qualified people!

This newly expanded edition is filled with general guiding principles and nitty-gritty details. It contains fifty new pages of insights and illustrative examples from films across the globe, as well as helpful photos, important references and real-world examples. If I were to teach a college course on creating English subtitles, this book would be my only text.

The timing of *The Elements of Subtitles* could not be better. Never before have we Americans had such easy access to so many foreign films. There are literally thousands of highly entertaining and uplifting stories from Asia, Europe, Latin America, Africa, and the Middle East just waiting to be discovered. But our discovery hinges on the quality of the English subtitles associated with these productions. Having low-quality English subtitles on a magnificent foreign film is like being told we may watch Kurosawa Akira's witty *Yojimbo* (1961)—but only while someone with no sense of humor describes the plot. Or wearing someone else's scratched-up glasses while browsing a famous art gallery. We'd never allow it! But we are forced to sit through mediocre subtitles on foreign films all the time. And subtitles are the viewers' "eyeglasses" to see clearly into the film's original intent.

I would say that English subtitles on a majority of foreign films, especially from Asia, are average at best. It continues to amaze me how a production company will spend millions of dollars making a film and then not worry about the subtitle quality when the film is later distributed in the US and other countries. I've seen this example dozens of times:

- A foreign production company will sell the US distribution rights of a popular film to a US-based distribution company.
- The production company assumes that the US distributor is qualified to handle the English subtitles—in most cases, subtitles or "subtitle quality" are never mentioned during the negotiation stages.
- One of the employees at the US distribution company has a friend who speaks the foreign language and English. It's assumed that this bilingual person can crank out some English subtitles in no time. It can't be that difficult, right?

What I just described is a regular occurrence in the process of bringing foreign films with English subtitles to American audiences. English subtitle quality is often just an afterthought. This is akin to the New York Yankees asking a young man who can throw a baseball 100mph to pitch in their next game. Throwing hard doesn't make him a good pitcher. Likewise, just because someone can speak both the "source language" and the "target language" of a film does not mean that person is or will be a good subtitle translator.

Yojimbo (1961)

Subtitlers need training. They need the proper tools. They need guidance. They need to know the elements of subtitles. On page 164, Bannon writes:

> Subtitling is fun. It is thrilling to find just the right inflection, the perfect phrase that captures as much of the original as possible. . . . a translation that communicates what is said and unsaid is a wonder to behold.

If you are already in the subtitle translation field, then this book will help your skills go from good to great. If you are looking to start your career in this field, then this is the only book you will ever need. This newly expanded edition has all the elements, formulas, tools, and examples to help anyone who is truly interested in subtitling to create perfect phrases.

For the sake of foreign film lovers everywhere, I wish all subtitle translators—whether they work at a large translation agency or from home as part-time freelancers—would read this expanded edition.

Tom Larsen
YA Entertainment, LLC

Foreword to the First Edition

"Like crap through a goose"

If you've picked up this book, you obviously have an interest in non-native films and understand the difference between subtitles and dubbing. I won't bother to explain the two modes of translation. The true question here is why that difference is so important, what separates the two and why any of us should give a damn.

I've watched my fair share of foreign films. That's probably why the author of this book tapped my shoulder to write a foreword. It certainly doesn't make me an expert on subtitles but it *does* mean I know what I like. The next time you watch a home release of a foreign film, turn both subtitles and dubbing on. Watch them simultaneously and you'll see how vastly different they are.

The subtitled version always offers the more accurate translation. The dubbed version isn't really a translation at all. Most of the story is lost while the dubbers try to work within the timing of the actors' dialogue. I've seen entire subplots completely eliminated for the sake of lining up voices for American audiences. All because we like sound to match lip movements. Now, I am not belittling the talents of voice actors. Most of them are really quite good. But some movies have been terribly miscast and the dubbed versions don't even come close to the originals. *Kiki's Delivery Service* and *Project A-Ko* are perfect examples of this.

Dubbing forces a movie to become something it is not: *American*. By dubbing the films into English, we ignore the fact that these are indeed foreign films and should be viewed in their original languages. *La Femme Nikita*, *Brotherhood of the Wolf* or *Let The Right One In* are fantastic movies that I could never imagine watching dubbed. Why would you want to take a film's dialogue and hammer it into English? It steals the fun. It robs the audience of the actors' performances. It is truly a crime.

To me it doesn't get any worse than "crap through a goose". I've loved the Godzilla films since I first saw one in my early twenties. I can't blame childhood nostalgia for my infatuation. It's an adult-bred love. I've shared the joy with my two boys and even infected this book's author with the G-virus—don't let him deny it. But what does that have to do with fowl feces?

Takao Okawara's *Godzilla™ 2000 Millenium* (1999) was one of Toho's franchise re-launches after a small break from the Godzilla movies of the nineties. The film even had a limited theatrical release in the US. This is almost unheard of with a Godzilla movie. Of course, I ran out and watched it in a sadly empty theater. Americans apparently don't have much love for the King of Monsters—but that's another story. Toho Company, Ltd. is ferocious about protecting their properties from pirating or downloading. It's one of the few companies that sends representatives to the big conventions, such as the San Diego Comic-Con, to report bootleg vendors to the proper authorities. Unfortunately Toho doesn't protect its films against bad dubbing.

The TriStar US release of *Godzilla 2000* shows how dubbing serves up the original film "like crap through a goose". The dubbed adaptation of Hiroshi Kashiwabara and Wataru Mimura's screenplay dramatically changed the movie. It sounds wrong. It's inaccurate. It stinks like poultry poop.

GENERAL

As we know from experience, when Godzilla's attacked he advances instead of retreats. We can make use of his aggressiveness by luring him to the mouth of the river.

MITSUO KATAGIRI

And what happens once he gets there?

GENERAL

The underwater mines will do the rest.

POLITICIAN

Mines? What about the safety of the local residents?

GENERAL

Ah, yes. Well, I'm not saying we wouldn't get our hair mussed. But I can promise no more than two, three hundred tops.

POLITICIAN

I don't like it. And if the mines fail to stop him? Then what?

Godzilla (1954)

GENERAL

We've developed an advanced new weapon. A new generation of armor-piercing missile. It's so powerful it can penetrate any known material. I guarantee it will go through Godzilla like crap through a goose.

Like crap through a goose. I can't imagine that this is the term Toho would have chosen. Most likely some dubber thought the phrase was funny. The general is grizzled and tough, but he's no comic military cliché. Here's part of the same scene in subtitles from the Universal Laser release (Hong Kong, 2000):

POLITICIAN

What if Godzilla ignores us and heads for the nuclear power plant?

GENERAL

In that case, 'Blast bombs' buried in the ground will block Godzilla's way to the reactor.

POLITICIAN

Fine. You drive it down to the river. Then what?

GENERAL

We developed a new weapon especially for this day. It's a new type of full-metal missile that will penetrate anything, not just to blast it. It's totally different from conventional ones. It can drill Godzilla's skin, no matter how tough he is.

This version could use a better subtitler and a harsh edit, but at least it's accurate. In the film, Godzilla is serious business. The general is reporting to his civilian supervisor. I doubt goose excrement was on his mind. I'm not vilifying voice actors. If I give that impression, I apologize. But I *am* passionate about subtitles versus dubbing.

Subtitles present the film the way it was meant to be seen. They are more accurate than dubbing and—when done right—much more entertaining. We can actually enjoy the actors' performances as they brought them to the screen; sounds, images and all. There's no other way to see a foreign film. If people appreciated the hard work of subtitlers, we might avoid all the goose crap.

The next time you watch a foreign film at home and can choose between subtitles and dubbing, click subtitles. Sure, reading is a little more work. But the payoffs are so much bigger.

Troy Hasbrouck
Jester Press Comics

Introduction

Scope and Purpose

This book is written for the working subtitle translator. It uses translation examples and samples from the best screenplays. Whether the dialogue is good, bad or indifferent, this book covers how to make it work in subtitles that accurately represent the original's meaning, intent and unique character. It is assumed that the subtitler is fluent in the **source language** (the screenplay) and the **target language** (English). It is further assumed that the subtitler is conversant with basic rules of usage in both languages and hopes to deliver subtitles that are as compelling as the original film.

For all subtitlers. This book is designed for any translator working with English subtitles. Although the author specializes in Korean-to-English subtitles, the lessons are emphatically **not** limited to that language pair. The book is filled with examples from across the world.

Non-technical. Grammar, usage, capitalization, dots, line breaks and justification get considerable attention in the chapter on *Style*, but only as they apply to any subtitle translator working for any production company. Most firms have very specific technical requirements for characters per line and lines per screen, but these change from business to business. Spotting—marking the beginning and end of spoken dialogue according to the film's timecode—can vary greatly between production companies. Each of the three firms with which the author most frequently works observes dramatically different technical protocols. One prefers its own proprietary software, the next MS Word, the last Excel. One has very rigid lines-per-second rules, another hardly any rules at all. The lessons of this book are designed to fit any timing and space requirements. Technical specifications come and go, but good subtitles never change.

Pedagogy. The author is a working translator but not a translation scholar. Theories of identity, equivalence, invisibility, domestication/foreignization, fidelity/infidelity and control deserve careful study, but are not addressed as such in this book. A practical guide is just that—practical.

Proper Tools

A working computer, a reliable high-speed internet connection and industry-standard spreadsheet and word processor programs are essential. The translator's preferred dictionary is a valuable tool, but not the only one. Reference material relevant to the content of the script is also helpful.

Source material. The masters on disc and the shooting script are essential to a quality translation. Masters provide clean, clear audio and video. Shooting scripts are often different from what ultimately aired but are still useful. They provide a sense of plot structure and clues to what is said when the audio is garbled or an actor mumbles.

The Approach of this Book

It is an irony of subtitles that many English equivalents are more accurate than purely literal translations. Three of the most common subtitling approaches:

Adaptation. Some firms hire a translator and a script adaptor. Dubbing projects frequently go this route.

> **Pro:** Done well, the result seems to match the original perfectly.
> **Con:** Dialogue is often widely divergent from the source.

Literal. With entertainment, "literal" usually means English subtitles written in the structure of the original. Literal does not always mean accurate.

> **Pro:** Confidence that the original's *structure* remains intact.
> **Cons:** Cumbersome, awkward phrasing and often over long.

Non-literal equivalent. Many distributors take a middle ground. The subtitles are as literal as possible, but idiomatic equivalents are used to ensure the primary goal: a seemingly effortless entertainment that captures the nuances and intent of the source.

> **Pros:** Reads like natural dialogue. This approach honors the original intent while maintaining a colloquial flavor.
> **Con:** English equivalents are not exact. No translation is.

This book leans toward non-literal equivalents in most examples.

Chapter One

Dialogue

NICK

I'm a hero. I was shot twice in the *Tribune*.

NORA

I read you were shot five times in the tabloids.

NICK

It's not true. He didn't come anywhere near my tabloids.

—*The Thin Man* (1934)

Subtitles are unlike any other type of translation. They present words in a new medium. Dubbing translates audio to audio, as does interpreting. Literary translation moves text from one written form to another. Subtitles cross linguistic and media barriers. They replicate the style and intent of spoken dialogue as words on a screen. Viewers immersed in the sounds and images of a film rely on subtitles to bridge these sensory perceptions. Subtitling is a remarkable endeavor with its own unique challenges and rewards, as observed by Atom Egoyan and Ian Balfour:

> Subtitles offer a way into worlds outside of ourselves. They
> are a unique and complex formal apparatus that allows the
> viewer an astounding degree of access and interaction.
> Subtitles embed us.

Good subtitles don't just transfer words from one language to another. They are as funny, scary, witty and compelling as the original. Success is measured by how little viewers notice them. That is the goal—to be completely transparent.

Abé Mark Nornes, Chair of the Department of Screen Arts & Culture and Professor in Asian Languages and Cultures at the University of Michigan, advises filmmakers to acquaint themselves with how translations affect their films in the international market. Nornes' questions raise important points for subtitlers:

> So film artists should learn about translation and find out who these people are. What do they actually know about cinema in the first place? What do they understand about narrative? Performance? Sound? History? The majority of translators see their task as nothing other than the transference of meaning from one language to another. . . . That is to say, the craft of the screenplay routinely goes unacknowledged. The tools of the screenwriter—things like foreshadowing, alliteration, metaphor, vulgarity, and so on—go largely untouched by translators striving for the anonymously straightforward prose of the subtitle or dubbing. In subtitling, the craft of the actor, with its timing, force, and volume, goes similarly ignored. If the studios demanded this kind of reduction and restraint of their artists, the creative unions would strike in an instant!

Translation is adaptation. A translator must understand the original's intent, the meaning behind the words. Time and space constraints often require clever solutions and no small amount of wit on the subtitler's part to ensure the viewers enjoy what's on the screen. This is especially difficult with languages that have vastly different grammatical structures and colloquial traditions. Dialogue should flow as smoothly and naturally as it does in the original. In the best translations viewers remember the subtitles as though the characters had actually spoken them in English.

The Importance of Dialogue

The importance of studying dialogue cannot be overstated. A subtitler must study the natural rhythm and tone of each speaker in a film; then find an equivalent tone in English. The best films are primers for the subtitle professional, as stressed by Japanese film director Kurosawa Akira:

> In order to write scripts, you must first study the great novels and dramas of the world. You must consider why they are great. Where does the emotion come from that you feel as you read them? What degree of passion did the author have to have, what level of meticulousness did he have to command, in order to portray the characters and events as he did? You must read thoroughly, to the point where

you can grasp all these things. You must also see the great films. You must read the great screenplays.

Well-written characters sound right. Some are wittier than others, perhaps, but the best screenplays ring true. Dashiell Hammett's dialogue for Sam Spade was lifted from the novel to director John Huston's script of *The Maltese Falcon* (1941). Spade has decided to turn Brigid O'Shaughnessy in to the police:

> I hope they don't hang you, precious, by that sweet neck. Yes, angel, I'm gonna send you over. The chances are you'll get off with life. That means if you're a good girl, you'll be out in 20 years. I'll be waiting for you. If they hang you, I'll always remember you.

Hammett's dialogue is fresh, incisive and an excellent example of economy in writing. Later in the same scene:

SPADE

All we've got is that maybe you love me and maybe I love you.

BRIGID

You know whether you love me or not.

SPADE

Maybe I do. I'll have some rotten nights after I've sent you over, but that'll pass.

No one in film history talks like Sam Spade. "When you're slapped you'll take it and like it," he says. Fictional worlds have rules of their own. In *The Maltese Falcon* Spade's dialogue is pitch perfect. At their best, subtitles carry the same unique flavor as the original. A viewer could pause a film and immediately know which character is speaking just by the style of the words on the screen. It's not easy, but for the translator, it's worth the effort. Films are entertainment. Their subtitles should be entertaining.

The Maltese Falcon (1941)

Natural, Faux Natural & Unnatural Voice

> With a good script a good director can produce a master-piece; with the same script a mediocre director can make a passable film. But with a bad script even a good director can't possibly make a good film.
>
> —Kurosawa Akira

There is little subtitles can do to help a stinker. Generally the programs chosen for export are of good quality, but not always. There is much that is altruistic and noble in helping to bridge cultures, but to viewers there is really only one goal: enjoy the film. This may not be easy. Subtitlers frequently encounter programs for which they have no enthusiasm whatsoever. Hack writing, poor dialogue, dull plots or a topic that doesn't appeal. It's inevitable but not crippling. Consider Ray Charles' observations on musical genres:

> You got country, you got jazz, you got classical music—all kinds of music. When you think about it you got many branches of music, but there's only two kinds of music in the world. There's good and bad. That's it. And it's true. It's so true. You see, you can find great music in all walks of life. You just have to take your time and really listen to it, 'specially if it's some music that you're not accustomed to. Because if you find an abundance of people that like that kind of music, you can be sure it has some kind of meaning for them, it may not be your type of music, but if you really stop and analyze it, really listen to it, you can understand.

Most films that find international distribution had a large fan base in their country of origin. For whatever reason, people enjoyed the show. Distributors are hoping it will have the same appeal in other countries. The translator's job is to identify the plot, character and dialogue elements that resonated with the original viewers and communicate them to the new target audience. Someone will wander into a store, read the back, and think, "Hmm, sounds interesting, I'll give it a whirl." Translate for that person.

The Unnatural World of Fiction

"Write what you know" is poor advice for screenwriters and translators. If every writer followed this time-worn teaching, the world would be filled with movies about struggling writers. Better to dream, as Shirley Jackson candidly admitted: "I personally love writing. It is a logical extension of the adolescent daydream . . . most clearly a way of making daily life into a wonderfully unusual thing instead of a grind."

Filmgoers can be grateful that despite having never been struck by an empire or raided a lost ark, Lawrence Kasdan managed to write scripts that thrill and move us. The best films create a world of their own. The dialogue created for them has its own cadence and foibles. They are unnatural, as explained by Dean Koontz:

> Many writers think—erroneously—that fiction should be a mirror or reality. Actually, it should act as a sifter to refine reality until only the essence is before the reader. This is nowhere more evident than in fictional dialogue. In real life, conversation is often roundabout, filled with general commentary and polite rituals. In fiction, the characters must always get right to the point when they talk.

Gangster films typify this kind of natural speech in an unnatural world. They are rich with unique speech patterns. Study the best writers of the genre, such as Elmore Leonard. Director Barry Sonnenfeld's *Get Shorty* (1995) went into production with a bland screenplay that wasted the remarkable dialogue of Leonard's original novel—the same way some subtitles can ruin a great script. John Travolta, who played Chili Palmer in the film, explained to *TIME Magazine* that he insisted on Leonard's dialogue. He used an example from the novel when Palmer's coat is stolen from a check room:

> You see a black leather jacket, fingertip length, has lapels like a suitcoat? You don't, you owe me three seventy-nine. . . . You get the coat back or you give me the three seventy-nine my wife paid for it at Alexander's.

The screenplay, on the other hand, translated Palmer's dialogue to:

> Where's my coat? You better find it. It cost $400.

Ultimately, Travolta said, "they put every goodie back." This is an example of the difference between functional dialogue and words that have a life of their own. Early in the film, Palmer says, "I'm not gonna say any more than I have to, if that." The addition of "if that" gives the character a natural speaking style in the movie's unnatural world. The subtitle translator must try to honor and replicate the rich flavor of the original. A daunting task. Many American writers have tried to replicate Leonard's style with no success. If a film is particularly well-written, the translator may not be able to reproduce the effortless and witty dialogue exactly—but the subtitles can give as good an approximation as possible. Consider director David Mamet's wickedly funny script for *Heist* (2001). Two criminals are discussing a job. One says he doesn't need the money. The other replies:

> Everybody needs money! That's why they call it money!

Dialogue doesn't come better than that. Mamet's *House of Games* (1987), from a story by Mamet and Jonathan Katz, is filled with the rhythms US audiences have come to recognize as belonging to con artists:

> The basic idea is this. It's called a confidence game. Why?
> Because you give me your confidence? No. Because I give
> you mine.

The character, Mike, illustrates his point by offering trust to his mark. In a Western Union office he acts as though he's waiting on some money. A marine asks after his wire; he needs it to buy a bus ticket. In the ensuing con, the grifter convinces the marine that they're comrades ("You're in the Corps? I was in the Corps."); then offers the young man money for his ticket. The marine refuses, but when his wire comes in, he offers the grifter cash. Mike never once asked for anything. He gave his confidence. This giving and taking of trust is a major theme in the film that comes up frequently, though subtly, in dialogue. Near the end, the grifter betrays the female protagonist in one of Mamet's great lines: "Ooh, you're a bad pony. And I'm not gonna bet on you." Compare the wit of Mamet and Leonard with the heavier, danger-laden dialogue of Mario Puzo's adaptation of his own novel, *The Godfather* (1972), directed by Francis Ford Coppola. Bonasera comes to Don Corleone for a favor:

BONASERA

I went to the police, like a good American.

DON CORLEONE

Why did you go to the police? Why didn't you come to me first?

BONASERA

I didn't want to get into trouble.

DON CORLEONE

Bonasera, Bonasera, what have I ever done to make you treat me so disrespectfully? If you'd come to me in friend-ship, this scum who ruined your daughter would be suffer-ing this very day. And if by some chance an honest man like yourself made enemies, they would become my ene-mies. And then, they would fear you.

Puzo's adaptation for the screen takes excellent dialogue and makes it nearly perfect. The same excerpt from Don Corleone as it reads in the novel:

But if you had come to me, my purse would have been yours. If you had come to me for justice those scum who ruined your daughter would be weeping bitter tears this day. If by some misfortune an honest man like yourself made enemies they would become my enemies... and then, believe me, they would fear you.

Neither version is better than the other. Both communicate a sense of Don Corleone appropriate to the medium. Both serve as examples of how much difference small changes in dialogue can make to subtitles. Were this being translated from, say, Sicilian, the subtitler must decide which excerpt is best— just as Puzo chose one version for his novel and another for film.

Good dialogue is found treasure to many translators who can't wait to rise to the challenge of putting it in subtitles. The 2007 television crime thriller, *Time Between Dog & Wolf* is a solid example. In this scene from Episode 12, undercover officer Suhyun has lost his memory and taken on the persona of Kay, right-hand man to crime boss Mao. The literal translation:

KAY

How much do you trust me? Do you think I will always stay with you?

MAO

Why are you asking me this all of a sudden?

KAY

A little while ago a National Intelligence Service officer contacted me privately.

MAO

NIS?

KAY

Yes. It appears there was an NIS officer that died who looked like me. After the NIS learned about my amnesia, they tried to use that death to bring me to their side. He said that I and that man are the same person.

MAO

Anyway, they didn't bring you to their side. If they succeeded, you wouldn't have told me this.

KAY

I'm sorry.

MAO

What are you sorry for? If it bothers you, you want me to look into it?

KAY

Sir, if you trust me then I'm fine. I'll take care of it.

MAO

OK. Kay...

KAY

Yes, sir?

MAO

Men who have experienced almost dying together don't need things like trust. Because they are one.

The original dialogue is wonderful. This literal translation is tremendously bad. It lacks the rhythm of the original and the pathos of two men talking about the most important thing in their lives—loyalty:

KAY

You think I'm a stand up guy? A guy that sticks with you to the end?

MAO

Where'd this come from?

KAY

The NIS contacted me. In secret.

MAO

The NIS?

KAY

Yes, sir. Seems I look like some guy killed in the line of duty. I figure they heard about my amnesia and want to use it to make me betray the Triad. They're saying I'm this dead guy.

MAO

Well, it didn't work, did it? I mean, it worked, we wouldn't be having this conversation.

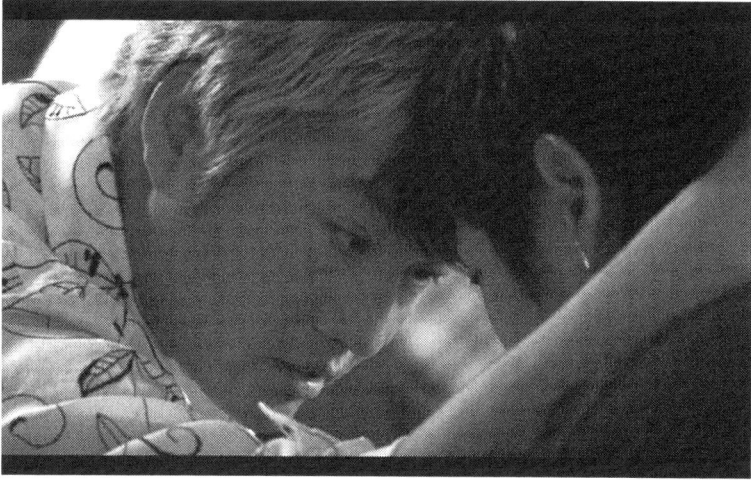

Time Between Dog & Wolf (2007)

KAY

I'm sorry, sir.

MAO

For what? Want I should look into it?

KAY

You trust me, that's all I need. I'll handle it.

MAO

Good. And Kay...

KAY

Yes, sir.

MAO

Guys like us, that almost died together, we don't need trust.
We got each other.

The original script did the scene justice. A translation should attempt to capture the cadence of the scene, the insights it provides, and the tone and style of the dialogue. This translation gives viewers a sense of the original script. The cadence and rhythm match the breath points in the dialogue and capture the feel of films in the genre. It allows viewers to immerse themselves in the characters. It feels natural in the unnatural world created by the program.

Combining Natural and Unnatural Dialogue

Subtitles must find the balance between natural and unnatural dialogue. It takes time and knowledge of the best screenplays, as well as understanding of the source material. Three steps to finding the right tone in subtitles:

1. Learn speech patterns appropriate to the characters.
2. Study the rhythms and nuances of the natural language created in the fictional world of the script.
3. Recreate the dialogue of the screenplay's unnatural fictional world while giving the characters voices that are true to type.

Avoiding Faux Natural Voice

Lesser films are frequently burdened by faux natural voice—dialogue that sounds false in the scene and reads poorly in subtitles. It is glib and forced, as in this snippet from a US ad campaign (company name changed): "I'm chilling with my homeboys at the Gas-n-Sip digging my favorite burger." This is terrible dialogue. Such breezy affectations rarely resonate in subtitles.

When in doubt, use standard phrasing. When it's not clear if a character might say "You want I should look into it?" or "You want me to look into it?" choose the latter. Better to be bland than to hit the wrong note.

Know what the dialogue is about. There may be bits of foreshadowing or references to obscure cultural items. Know what the characters are saying or the subtitles will be as confused as the translator. This can be tricky with screenplays that enjoy playing with words. The translator must understand the full context of the dialogue and its allusions.

Be as clear as the original—and as ambiguous. Once the translator is certain what the dialogue is about, the subtitles can accurately include the subtle foreshadowing or hints of the original without giving anything away. If the character says, "I'm going upstairs because I heard a noise," fine, write it. But if he says, "I'll be right back" and walks upstairs, write no more than that. If the context is clear, be as clear in the subtitles. Be aware of the screenplay's intentional ambiguity and honor it. Resist adding anything. David Mamet's advice to actors applies equally to subtitlers:

> Most actors try to use their intellectuality to portray the idea of the movie. Well, that's not their job. Their job is to accomplish, beat by beat, as simply as possible, the specific action set out for them by the script and the director.

Use nouns and verbs. When the subtitles seem to be lost in the maze of a really long sentence that doesn't seem to end no matter how many words are written... simplify. Break the sentence into parts. Delete unnecessary words.

Avoid unnecessary adverbs and adjectives. Dialogue in the source language may be filled with cumbersome descriptors. "The beautiful woods are dark in the deep winter," reads a translation of Robert Frost. Prefer the poet's vigorous voice: "The woods are lovely, dark and deep."

Simple is best—space constraints. Time and space are at a premium in subtitles. If the original has too many layers to communicate effectively, choose the gist of the meaning and move on. This goes against the grain, but ultimately nothing will work if the words don't fit on the screen.

Longer is clearer—beware brevity. If space allows, use it to share the nuances of the dialogue with the viewer. Brevity has its place, but brief subtitles run the risk of being bland—and losing important subtleties.

Internal voice. It's unlikely a writer has experienced all of the scenes and feelings that come up in film and television. The subtitler may not know what it's like to talk like a 90-year-old African American enduring racism or a 10-year-old orphan with superpowers. But every writer has an internal voice that resonates when a phrase is just right. Trust it.

Avoid Line-by-Line Translations

Line-by-line translations are often cumbersome and sometimes nonsensical. When a character is discussing a point within a paragraph, the translator may choose to shorten the phrasing by referring to the main point with a pronoun after it has been introduced. This is illustrated in the following literal translation from Episode 33 of *East of Eden*. Observe how Myung-hoon's dialogue buckles under its own weight.

> Don't you see the wounds on my body? It is because your
> son nearly died at the hands of his father.

The second line, in particular, is an excellent example of how the original may have been perfect for the character's mood and extreme angst, but falls flat in English. The power of the moment is lost. Better to express the character's tremendous sense of betrayal directly:

> See these wounds? I got them 'cause you nearly killed me.

That phrasing is short enough for subtitles, it fits the timing of the scene, and is an English equivalent of the tone and style of this important confrontation. Another scene demonstrates the need to find emphatic phrasing that communicates the character's mood and tone within the time and space allotted for subtitles. Two characters discuss Myung-hoon's father, Shin Tae-hwan. The viewer is struck by the Dong-chul's directness, despite the pain his words cause. A literal translation sounds forced:

DONG-CHUL

Only Shin Tae-hwan could do this.

MYUNG-HOON

How... what proof do you have?

DONG-CHUL

Because I know his heart. No, I know ALL of his heart.

The phrasing is powerful in the original language. It leaves no room for argument. But the literal translation is more appropriate to comedy—in English it doesn't work. The challenge, then, is to find similar English phrasing that makes the point without equivocation or odd dialogue. To do this, the subtitles substitute "proof" for "heart." This is an important point. The character says "heart" twice, but that sounds hollow. Rewriting "heart" as mind or guts comes off as silly. Viewers should get a sense of the original's repetitive dialogue style:

DONG-CHUL

Only Tae-hwan would try something like this.

MYUNG-HOON

What... proof do you have?

DONG-CHUL

The proof is that I know him. I know what he's capable of.

The literal translation is "because I know," but here the repetition "I know" is a solid example of how literal phrasing may be blended into context. Equally, "I know what he's capable of" is exactly the type of thing this character would say in English, in the same tone and body language, in this situation. And there is no doubt that it is the best English equivalent of "I know ALL of his heart." Think carefully about each line: space, timing, context and character. Non-literal translations must use English equivalents that are true to the tone and style of the dialogue.

Common Dialogue Challenges

You will see that this little clicking contraption with the revolving handle will make a revolution in our life—in the life of writers. It is a direct attack on the old methods of literary art. We shall have to adapt ourselves to the shadowy screen and to the cold machine. *A new form of writing will be necessary.*

—Leo Tolstoy

Not every program imported for US audiences is filled with great dialogue. The author of this book is a Godzilla fan, but despite the beast's undeniable place in film history, it's unlikely the movies will make anyone's Top Ten Scripts list. Some 1970s Godzilla films seem to revel in their own badness. Translating them can be a hoot. It's a long hard haul to shape mediocrity into endurable subtitles. Every subtitler faces bad dialogue, sooner or later.

Circular Dialogue

    A: He is my brother.
    B: He's your brother?
    A: Yes, my brother. We're related.
    B: By blood? Like brothers?

There's no helping this kind of dialogue. It goes round and round, scene after scene. Usually the intent seems to be to beat home an important plot point.

Retread. Another type of circular dialogue is the retread. The audience has watched an important scene. A few minutes later, one character is telling another a play-by-play of what just happened. The audience knows this and there's no reason to listen to it again, other than as filler. Better screenplays simply have the character say something like, "We need to talk," and cut to the next scene, trusting that the audience infers the essential points have been covered in off-screen dialogue.

Fortunately, circular dialogue is relatively easy to translate. It rarely has anything new to offer. The subtitles should display any subtle variations in speech patterns and move on.

Expository Dialogue—Action

Expository dialogue is used to explain characters—how they talk about themselves and others—and to describe actions and events not seen on-screen. Emmy Award-winning producer and author Kate Wright:

> Using *expository dialogue to set forth the literal meaning or expressed purpose of the scene* is deadly. If you find yourself 'staging' scenes with people talking to one another, or making confessions to one another, you are headed in the wrong direction. . . . Expository dialogue is the ultimate no-no!

This typifies expository dialogue that describes off-screen action:

> A: It's a good thing Leroy bet $10K on that horse. Or we wouldn't have the money to drive across Arizona today.
> B: Yes, Granny Smith was glad to see us when we stopped in Tucson. Can't wait to get to California.

Painful to watch, excruciating to translate, expository dialogue is a necessary evil. There are certain essential bits of information that the audience must know to understand what comes later. Gifted writers work it in when needed and leave much out, trusting in the audience's intelligence, as observed by Pulitzer Prize winning novelist Wallace Stegner: "Never explain too much; a reader is offended if he cannot participate and use his mind and imagination, and a story loses much of its suspense the moment everything is explained."

Unlike circular dialogue, expository dialogue often contains vital intelligence. Note how much useful information is revealed in Lawrence Kasdan's vigorous screenplay for *Raiders of the Lost Ark* (1981):

MAJOR EATON

Doctor Jones, we've heard a lot about you.

INDIANA

Have you.

EATON

Professor of Archeology. Expert on the occult and how does one say it? Obtainer of rare antiquities.

INDIANA

That's one way of saying it.

[*later in the same scene*]

EATON

You see for the last two years the Nazis have had teams of archeologists running around the world looking for all sorts of religious artifacts. Hitler's gone nuts on the subject. He's crazy. He's obsessed with the occult. And right now, apparently, there is some kind of German archeological dig going on in the desert outside Cairo.

COL MUSGROVE

Now we have some information here but we can't make anything out of it and maybe you can. 'Tannis development proceeding. Acquire headpeace, Staff of Ra, Abner Ravenwood, US.'

INDIANA

The Nazis have discovered Tannis!

EATON

Now just what does that mean to you? Tannis.

INDIANA

Tannis is one of the possible resting places of the Lost Ark.

COL. MUSGROVE

The Lost Ark?

INDIANA

Yeah, the Ark of the Covenant. The chest the Hebrews used to carry the Ten Commandments around in.

EATON

Alright, now, what do you mean the Ten Commandments, you talking about THE Ten Commandments?

INDIANA

Yes, the actual Ten Commandments; the original stone tablets that Moses came down out of Mount Horeb and smashed if you believe in that sort of thing. Didn't you guys ever go to Sunday School? Look, the Hebrews took the broken pieces and put them into the Ark. When they settled in Canaan they put the Ark in a place called the Temple of Solomon where it stayed for many years. 'Till all of a sudden, whoosh, it was gone.

This is all the exposition needed to launch into one exciting adventure after another. It is presented with economy. The scene would be hindered by editorial asides or bracketed explanations of Mt. Horeb or the Temple of Solomon. Those types of *explainers* are a little silly.

Explainers—original screenplay. Typified by lines dubbed-in after filming. For example, a group is leaving a bar late at night. The action speaks for itself, but then the audience hears an oddly canned voice as one of the characters mutters, "Let's go home." In another program, the power goes off in a large building. A character flips open her cell and barks, "Get the generator running!" It wasn't necessary to call the maintenance crew. Chances are they knew what to do. This explainer alerted viewers that the building had a back-up generator. Explainers stop the flow of the program. They are reminiscent of Humphrey Bogart's advice on acting: "If a guy points a gun at you the audience knows you're afraid. You don't have to make faces." Or make explainers.

Explainers—subtitles. It's tempting to use a word from the source language as a teaching tool about the culture or history of the country from which the film originated. Or to insert an editorial note in brackets. Both are a disservice to the viewer. They take the viewer out of the fictional world, drawing attention to the subtitler. Better to let the dialogue speak for itself. Remember translator Michael Hamburger's advice:

> To me it's not so much a question of liberties but of whether the translator is trying to impose himself on the text or whether he is trying to render the text. In order to render the text one must take liberties, but there is a difference here between somebody who simply uses the text as a springboard for his own exercises and inventions and somebody who is thinking primarily in terms of the text he's translating.

Expository dialogue often poses a problem for the translator: the information can seem entirely unrelated to the action on the screen or any previous conversations. Ways to meet this challenge:

- Read the entire screenplay.
- Double-check the seemingly unrelated bits.
- Translate the expository dialogue without giving anything away. This is harder than it sounds.

Dialogue that Sounds the Same

Pity the screenwriter who crafts sparkling dialogue only to be told by sponsors or producers that they prefer a more uniform feel. From clever to banal in just a few pen strokes. When faced with characters that sound the same, look for subtle ways the screenwriter or actors managed to liven up otherwise dull dialogue. Perhaps an inflection here, a verb there, that gives the character some sense of individuality. The translator can legitimately exploit these nuances to give the subtitles unique voices.

Verbs

Verbs and nuances of inflection play crucial roles in translating many subtitles. They should be handled with great care, respecting the intent as well as the literal phrasing. For example, at the end of *East of Eden*, the ghost of Lee Dong-chul tells his family that he loves them. First, to his wife and their child, he uses an intimate verb. Then he uses a standard familiar verb ending for the same word ("love") to encompass the rest of his family. Finally, he uses a formal verb ending to include his family and, it may be inferred, the viewers:

> I love you.
> All of you.
> I love you.

In the source dialogue, "love" is repeated in all three sentences. This repetition is presented in the subtitles as "I love you" twice, with "All of you" inserted to communicate the subtle difference in phrasing. The final "I love you" need not be subtitled differently. It is delivered directly into the camera. The change in tone and body language is clear to the viewer.

Out-of-Character Dialogue

An uneducated but savvy mountain man probably wouldn't say, "To which road do you refer?" nor would a stereotypical literature professor be likely to grumble, "What road you talkin' 'bout?" A translator works hard to match subtitles to character profiles, but sometimes the screenplay doesn't help. If the professor has used proper grammar throughout the program, but suddenly slips into a country accent for one or two lines, examine the plot. Is there a reason for this lapse? If so, it must be translated with that reason in mind.

Changing a character for the plot—original screenplay. It happens in even the best programs. An unlikely plot point is forced on a character. These actions don't fit the characters as they were written prior to the *faux pas*. The screenplay sacrifices character to plot. The translator must decide to fit the subtitles to the out-of-character dialogue, or to the tone and style viewers have come to expect from that character. To be safe, translate with standard phrasing.

Changing a character to show-off—subtitler. A particularly well-turned phrase pops into the translator's head. It's great for subtitles. A gem. But it doesn't fit any of the characters. No one in the entire film speaks that way. And the subtitler sticks it in anyway. Most working translators know the temptation to show-off is common and very human. It happens everyday, most often in vulgar expressions: a plethora of scatological wit, for example. Translators do indeed have specialized knowledge. It's fun to share it with others. Don't show off. Resist, resist, resist. The viewers will be grateful.

Stilted Dialogue

Literal translations almost always sound stilted. If the original dialogue is awkward and the translator honors this, the subtitles appear poor and hinder enjoyment of the film. This happens most often with minor characters. Pity the writer who had to pound it out (likely under deadline) and the actor who had to say it (probably glad to have the gig). And pity the poor viewers who have to read it in subtitles. To compensate for the occasional lapse in an otherwise good script consider keeping a formal tone without the stilted style:

> I think you are a handsome man and I enjoy sitting in this
> room with you here tonight.

This line can legitimately be translated in a tone that is still slightly formal, without the cumbersome phrasing:

> You're handsome. I'm glad we're together tonight.

Wordplay

Wordplay is particularly challenging for non-native speakers of a given language. Humor often thrives on variations and intricacies like those in the old vaudeville standard *Who's On First?*. Imagine the struggling translator in Outer Mongolia trying to subtitle Abbott & Costello:

ABBOTT

The Yankee's manager gave me a job as coach for as long
as you're on the team.

COSTELLO

If you're the coach, you must know all the players.

ABBOTT

I certainly do.

COSTELLO

Well you know I've never met the guys. So you'll have to
tell me their names, and then I'll know who's playing on the
team.

Bud Abbott and Lou Costello (1945)

ABBOTT

Oh, I'll tell you their names, but you know it seems to me they give these ball players now-a-days very peculiar names.

COSTELLO

You mean funny names?

ABBOTT

Strange names, pet names... Let's see, we have on the bags, Who's on first, What's on second, I Don't Know is on third...

COSTELLO

That's what I want to find out.

ABBOTT

I say Who's on first, What's on second, I Don't Know's on third.

COSTELLO

Are you the manager?

ABBOTT

Yes.

COSTELLO

You gonna be the coach too?

ABBOTT

Yes.

COSTELLO

And you don't know the fellows' names?

ABBOTT

Well I should.

COSTELLO

Well then who's on first?

ABBOTT

Yes.

COSTELLO

I mean the fellow's name.

ABBOTT

Who.

COSTELLO

The guy on first.

ABBOTT

Who.

COSTELLO

The first baseman.

ABBOTT

Who.

COSTELLO

The guy playing...

ABBOTT

Who is on first!

COSTELLO

I'm asking YOU who's on first.

ABBOTT

That's the man's name.

COSTELLO

That's who's name?

ABBOTT

Yes.

COSTELLO

Well go ahead and tell me.

ABBOTT

That's it.

COSTELLO

That's who?

ABBOTT

Yes.

Double Entendre. Many words have multiple meanings (polysemy) or they sound alike (homonymy). Both frequently rear their heads in comic double entendre—a translator's nightmare. It's hard enough to fit a single meaning in the space available. Usually multiple meanings are subtle and flash by quickly, as with the playful boudoir dialogue between newlyweds Jeanette MacDonald and Ramon Novarro in *The Cat and the Fiddle* (1934):

> SHIRLEY
>
> Ah. I had such a lovely dream. I dreamed of you all night.
>
> VICTOR
>
> Tell me.
>
> SHIRLEY
>
> I dreamed we were so rich you went around in a golden jacket.
>
> VICTOR
>
> And nothing else?
>
> SHIRLEY
>
> I don't think so.

This is classic bait-and-switch double entendre. At first, viewers infer "And nothing else?" means, "You didn't dream anything else?" Shirley's coy response gives it a second meaning. Ah-ha, the audience chuckles, he meant "And I was *wearing* nothing else?"

Double meanings double the frustration. And the rewards. Some languages have "counters" that identify the exact nature of an item being counted. These counters can lead to humorous wordplay, as in Episode 4 of *I Really, Really Like You*. The heroine is at the police station, mispronouncing words and dropping double meanings right and left. She uses a bit of double entendre with the counting term for cabbages. In the source language, "giving up" is pronounced *pogi*. This term is also used exclusively to count cabbages, so rather than say, "1 cabbage, 2 cabbages..." one would use the counting term, "1 *pogi*, 2 *pogi*, 3 *pogi*..." As a joke, Koreans mix the terms, saying, "The only time I use the word *pogi* (give up) is when I *pogi* (count) cabbages." This pun can be translated as follows:

> Give up? You can never count me out. The only counting
> out I do is counting out cabbages.

Imagine editing the line above to "Give up? I never give up." It would fail to communicate the endearing wordplay of the original. This double entendre had a solution, but for every success there are a dozen that have to be edited to the basic function of the dialogue.

Jeanette MacDonald

Mismatched forms of address. *I Really Really Like You* also makes great use of the mismatched speech gag. Thinking Bong-sun might be the president's daughter, the gardener adopts a formal speech pattern, referring to her as "My Lady." The Korean term he uses, *agassi*, is really just "young lady" but as with all humor, the context gives it the laughs. In this program the term carries special meaning, similar to its use in the old Korean royal house. Therein is the joke. When a crusty lady cook hears the gardener using this style of speech toward pretty Bong-sun in Episode 7, she accuses him of being some kind of deviant. Since the girl is so much younger, an informal style of speech would be appropriate in Korean society. The gardener's use of "My Lady" and formal verbs makes the old cook wonder if he's hitting on the girl. "You really must be a perv," she says, "calling some young thing 'My Lady'." This misunderstanding would be immediately inferred by the original audience and a guaranteed laugh. To communicate the special tone of this term, the subtitles affect a formal style whenever it was used. In Episode 15, the gardener refers to a birthday celebration as "Lady Bong-sun's Day of Birth." The mistaken identity joke plays well when his son responds, "So what makes this chickenhead a Lady? And Day of Birth? It's her birthday, like anyone else."

Alliterative word play. There are many alliteration gags that work just as well in English. In Episode 6 of *My Wife is a Superwoman*, devoted husband Dal-su is moonlighting as a driver. After chauffeuring a lovely woman around town, he comes home late and is confronted by his wife:

DAL-SU

I went out for some air.

JI-AE

Not out for an affair?

The subtitles replicate the original dialogue's play on words. In the source language, the common expression for going out for air is similar to "getting a little wind," an easy translation that needs little explanation. The term "wind" is also a colloquialism for a player or one having an affair. The original dialogue uses the same terms (wind/wind); the subtitles capture this alliterative wordplay with air/affair.

Dialogue Flow

Subtitles should never interfere with the flow of the scene. They should be nothing other than solid translations that the viewer's eye can easily follow. Every word must tell. Each phrase must ring true. In the opening scene of Episode 33 of *East of Eden*, two characters are careening headlong in a dangerous car chase. One of the characters, Rebecca, is screaming in the heat of the moment. She reveals shocking truths. Space and time are at a premium in this scene. The subtitles must communicate the essence of her important revelation without being long or cumbersome:

> Listen carefully. Before you die, listen carefully!

This translation is literal and comes off as stiff and too long. In Korean it makes perfect sense, but in English it's unlikely that one would speak this way while rushing headlong to possible death. The dialogue continues:

> Before you die, listen carefully. You are not the blood son
> of Shin Tae-hwan. It's a blessing to you that you die know-
> ing Shin Tae-hwan is not your father.

A literal translation falls flat and fails completely. The last line, in particular, is just silly in English. It might be re-phrased as, "It's better that you die knowing he's not your father," but the phrasing is still awkward and would barely fit in the time and space allotted for the scene, which moves quickly. The translation does not fit the flow of the scene.

In a scene this fast, with words that will doubtless be repeated in flashback throughout the program, it's essential to get the important information to the viewers while remaining true to the context (car chase, screaming) and the character, who is terrified but still manipulative. A firm hand is needed to communicate the desperation and speed of the scenez;

> Listen to me. You deserve the truth. You're not Shin Tae-
> hwan's son. You need to know. He's not your real father.

Context and timing are essential elements in maintaining smooth dialogue. Don't allow the subtitles to distract from the film. Follow the pace of a scene; keep the subtitles in sync with its rhythms.

Cumbersome Phrasing

Subtitles that don't reflect the tone and style of the speaker are bad enough; phrasing seldom used in colloquial expression is worse. There are certain educated, refined or snobby characters that may use grammatically correct expressions, but for most dialogue, avoid cumbersome phrasing in favor of a smooth style of speech.

Formal	Colloquial
To whom are you speaking?	Who you talking to?
That's the man about whom I was speaking.	That's the guy I was telling you about.

Linguist Charles L. Barber explained:

> In grammar we can see the continuation, in small ways, of the long-term historical trend in English from synthetic to analytic, from a system that relies on inflexions to one that relies on word order and on grammatical words (prepositions, auxiliary verbs, etc.). For example, the form *whom* is dropping out of use, at any rate in speech, and *who* tends to be used in all positions. Admittedly, we still have to use *whom* after a preposition, as in 'To whom shall I give it?'; but in fact this is not what we say in ordinary speech—we say 'Who shall I give it to?'

Formal address has a place. The subtitler must decide which style suits a given scene. When a sentence seems too awkward, shave away the excess and write in the character's natural voice.

Non-uniform Spelling of Names and Places

This is perhaps the best reason to keep a bible or a table of information that is repeated throughout a program. Audiences are intelligent and adaptive. Once a specific spelling has been identified, even an unorthodox one, most viewers are willing to buy into it for the duration. Switching half-way stops a show dead.

Being too Repetitive

Many languages are contextual. Pronouns and personal names are all but absent. They must be inferred by the viewer. A literal translation is comic:

A: Where going?
B: Going bank.

Where is *he* going? Where am *I* going? You? We? It's not clear. He, she, they? The meaning can only be understood in the context of the scene itself and by the inflections and nuances of the dialogue. The problem is not which pronoun to choose—the translator is perfectly aware who's going where—but how to shorten the subtitles to match this rapid-fire patter. "Where is he going?" followed by "He's going to the bank" is oddly stilted and too repetitive. It reads like subtitles. Ideally, a short pronoun followed by an implied statement will suffice:

A: Where's he going?
B: The bank.

Repetition in Multiple Languages

Another danger in repetition is the multi-lingual scenes so frequent in international thrillers. Either the characters are repeating themselves in a second (or third) language, or an interpreter is doing it for them. But the subtitles are all in English. Within the context of the scene it may be obvious that the interpreter is merely repeating the dialogue, in which case little explanation is required. However, some scenes have so many characters speaking that the viewers may wonder if they are missing lines. Subtly alter similar lines to communicate the interpreter's role. Consider this exchange from Episode 13 of *The Time Between Dog & Wolf*:

SELLER

We've designed a completely new method of exchange.

INTERPRETER

They have a new method of exchange.

SELLER

Bidding starts at triple the usual cost.

INTERPRETER

The opening bid is three times the normal price.

BUYER

Think you could be just a little MORE greedy?

INTERPRETER

Isn't your offer a little steep?

SELLER

It's highly concentrated and priced accordingly.

INTERPRETER

The drug is in a concentrated form so it costs more.

Viewers of this scene are aware the interpreter is present. By varying the phrasing—as all interpreters must—the subtitles indicate which of the characters is speaking at any given moment.

Not being Repetitive Enough

Dialogue often relies on repetition. These are occasions when the subtitles must do the same. It's natural to want to phrase things differently from sentence to sentence—it's almost an editing compulsion—but that's rarely wise.

In *I Really, Really Like You*, a comic exchange needs repetition to get the joke across. The Korean word for room, *bang*, is used liberally in common speech. A Net Café is an "Internet Room", a comic book shop is a "comic room", a karaoke bar is a "song room", etc. The script plays on repetition of the term "room" in Episode 25 when Bong-ki asks Bong-sun to go out with him:

BONG-KI

How about a karaoke 'room'? Net Café 'room'? Comic book 'room'? Sauna room? Phone room, laundry room, any room, you name it.

BONG-SUN

Go to YOUR room.

Note how the subtitles introduce the room gag with quotation marks; then leave them off as the dialogue progresses. Later in the scene, viewers see the pay-off when Bong-sun agrees to go out:

Let's go. Any room is fine, so long as it's not this room.

This kind of humor falls flat without repetition. There are other times to keep the original's repetitive wordplay. Bong-sun is a mountain girl. Her dialogue has a down-home feel. She frequently repeats herself, as in the first episode when she demands, "Gift? What gift?" Subtitles that fail to include this endearing speech pattern cheat viewers of the character's rich dialogue.

Remain Hidden from View

Stay true to the text. Try to be as transparent as possible. Subtitling professional Henri Béhar observes: "The titles should subtly give people the impression that they are understanding the characters speaking, not reading words on the screen." Béhar calls these "subliminal subtitles":

Subtitling is a form of cultural ventriloquism, and the focus must remain on the puppet, not the puppeteer. Our task as subtitlers is to create subliminal subtitles so in sync with the mood and rhythm of the movie that the audience isn't even aware it is reading. We want *not* to be noticed. If a subtitle is inadequate, clumsy, or distracting, it makes everyone look bad, but first and foremost the actors and the filmmakers. It can impact the film's potential career.

Never show off. The viewers should never notice the subtitler's personality. The translator is invisible. Let the film tell the story. Let the plot explain itself. Never foreshadow events that are not in the dialogue. Never over-explain. Stay out of it.

Never insert opinion. The translator may have strong views on a subject covered in a film. Beware coloring words and phrases with personal views that are not in the screenplay. This includes gender stereotypes. When in doubt, follow the guidelines set by London's National Union of Journalists:

> There is no reason why girls and women should be generally characterized as emotional, sentimental, dependent, vulnerable, passive, alluring, mysterious, fickle, weak, inferior, neurotic, gentle, muddled, vain, intuitive. . . . Nor is there any reason why boys and men should be assumed to be dominant, strong, aggressive, sensible, superior, randy, decisive, courageous, ambitious, unemotional, logical, independent, ruthless.

If the stereotype is not in the source, beware inadvertently using language based on personal preconceptions. On the other hand, a screenplay may be riddled with opinion. Avoid editing particularly unappealing attitudes to make them more palatable. Never censor.

Stay out of the way. Mastery of the source and target languages gives a translator remarkable freedom to become immersed in the film. When the subtitler stays out of the way, every aspect of the production—script, performances, sounds, images—can influence and inform the translation. This is as true when adapting a script as it is for interpreting a role. From soprano Renée Fleming:

> Stepping into a role should be like getting into a car: you no longer have to be conscious of how to drive at this point, but only of where you're going. . . . There is a kind of suspension of thinking involved, as though there is so much inspiration and ease that it feels as if you're channeling the music rather than singing it. Reaching that place allows me, in a sense, to step out of the music's way and leave my mind free to discover new shadings in the role that I might have missed in the past.

Simplify. "He is here in our town in the auditorium down the street" may be exactly what the original dialogue says. It may be short in the source language, but it's too long for English subtitles. "He's down the street in the auditorium" is acceptable.

Choose inert words. Certain terms are commonly recognized and dismissed as proper by the viewer. They continue the dramatic flow. Alternatives break the rhythm of the scene. Mismatched phrases make viewers pause at the inappropriate usage. Military commanders demand, "Report," whereas business managers say, "Tell me what happened." Subordinates respond, "Yes, sir." This is as true in subtitles as it is in one of the most popular shows in television history, as explained by Peter Falk:

> The next thing that developed was Columbo's exquisite politeness. And this happened in the very first episode. I called all men 'Sir' and all women 'Ma'am.' I sprinkled 'No, sirs' and 'Yes, ma'ams' and 'I beg your pardons' all over the room. . . . If you ask me why, I couldn't explain it. In hindsight, I often said that Columbo was by nature a polite man from birth.

"Yes, ma'am" and "I beg your pardon" are inert. They flash across the screen and aren't read as much as absorbed by the viewers. They are expected. To replace "yes, sir" with "sure" or "you got it" interrupts the flow of the scene. It draws attention to the subtitles. If there is a purpose for the interruption in the source dialogue, colorful terms are required. If the acquiescence is merely responsive, choose inert phrasing.

Entertainment

Movies are fun. Films and television programs are often a delight to fans. But most subtitles are tepid—words on a screen with little more character than instructions in a cookbook. The theory seems to be that if brevity is better then bland is best. Consider Magnolia Home Entertainment's 2009 home release of Tomas Alfredson's *Let the Right One In* (2008), written by John Ajvide Lindqvist from his novel:

POLICEMAN

The police have many ways to find out if something's fishy. Remember the house that burned down in Ängby? A house that burned to the ground. They found someone in there. Dead, of course. In that case we knew it was arson because they person had been murdered. How could we know that? [*Oskar raises his hand*] Yes?

OSKAR

Because there wasn't any smoke in the lungs.

POLICEMAN

That's correct. How did you figure it out?

OSKAR

I read a lot.

POLICEMAN

What kind of books, I wonder?

OSKAR

Newspapers and things like that.

POLICEMAN

And now we can talk a little about drugs.

Compare the theatrical release as subtitled by Ingrid Eng:

POLICEMAN

The police have ways to determine foul play... Do you remember that fire in Ängby? A house burned down and a
body was found inside. We knew that the fire had been set
to conceal the fact that the person had been murdered be-
forehand. So, how could they know that? [*Oskar raises his
hand*] Well... Go ahead.

OSKAR

There was no smoke in the lungs of the person who died.

POLICEMAN

That's correct. Did you figure that out right now?

OSKAR

No, I read a lot...

POLICEMAN

What kind of books would that be?

OSKAR

Just books.

POLICEMAN

Okay... I'm going to talk to you about drugs.

There is a difference of only three words between the home release and the
theatrical subtitles. Yet the home release lacks charm. The words are utilitarian,
communicating basic information with little or no characterization. Eng's
subtitles match the pace of the scene and give a sense of the policeman's
"school presentation" persona and the subtly insecure yet assertive Oskar. The
translation trusts the audience. Subtitles must respect the appeal a film had in
its home country—and the joy it may give new viewers in English. Identify
how the audience felt after leaving the theater. Make certain the subtitles are
about nothing else.

Chapter Two

Character

XANDER

Yep. Vampires are real, lot of 'em live in Sunnydale, Willow'll fill you in.

WILLOW

I know it's hard to accept at first...

OZ

No, actually, it explains a lot.

—*Buffy the Vampire Slayer* (1997)

Much dialogue in film and television is written to explain or further the plot. It lacks a sense of wonder. Character-driven dialogue, on the other hand, approaches the plot sideways. It seems whimsical, at times irrelevant, yet always speaks to the characters themselves, revealing who they are and how they feel about what is happening to them. Sadly, in poorly-realized translations some of the best dialogue is distilled into mere plot points.

There is no question that subtitles must be clear and further the story. They should never get in the way of the viewer's enjoyment of the film. But subtitles can do much more. They can replicate the feel of the source. They can communicate as closely as possible the tone and intent of the dialogue. A translation filled with the nuances and emotions of the original lends authenticity to its character voices. The subtitles ring true.

Write a Bible

Television programs evolve and change over many episodes, as do their characters. Many screenplays have primary and sub-themes that are slowly developed during the run of the show. The translator should identify these themes to ensure that foreshadowing dialogue or subtle hints may be fully realized later. A subtitler should create tables for names, dates, places, catch-phrases, running gags—any information that's likely to be repeated. Orson Scott Card explains:

> When I wasn't creating a bible as I went along, I once changed a character's name between chapter 5 and chapter 15. I forgot that I made him an orphan and had him tele-phone his mother. I've changed a minor character's race. I've changed other characters' professions, I've changed my hero's hair color, age, height, birthday—it's easy to do when a character isn't the focus of the action or when a lot of pages have intervened.

This is as true with scripts as it is with novels. For home viewers, subtle mistakes from one year to another are painfully obvious. A program that aired over the course of many years may be watched in a single weekend. What took days to translate is viewed in a matter of hours. A bible isn't just a face-saving exercise. It provides insight into speech patterns. Profiles are essential to capture the tone, style and proper phrasing of each character within the context of a given scene.

BAR: Background, Age, Region

Do not ignore this simple exercise. It is an essential foundation upon which to build character profiles. When in doubt about phrasing, step up to the BAR.

Background. Include anything that might influence speech patterns: edu-cation, religion, personal traumas, prison, illness, wealth (and lack of it), friends, travel, gender, everything that is said and unsaid in the script.

Age. People change over the years. Disregard stereotypes like the crotchety granny or the kind-hearted grandpa. Dig deeper. A retired gentleman in a film set in the late 1960s may have seen the Depression and served in World War II. Consider how this influences his speech patterns. The dialogue must fit his current status in life as well as the phrasing and usage of his formative years. Equally, a younger character will likely have a looser, more disjointed way of talking. The only rules are those created by the screenplay, but they exist and must be observed. Combine the age of the character with the background to find the right note for any subtitle line.

Region. Dialect plays an important part. As do accents and the atmosphere of the region in which the film is set as well as the years prior. For example, an African-American jazz singer that grew up in 1930s Georgia may live in Paris during the main action of the program. Her phrasing and inflection will be shaped by her past and current situations. These may be in the dialogue and should be in the subtitles.

Motivations

What does the character want? Or need? Defining a character's motivations makes the translation process much simpler. It helps in deciding what to leave in and what must be edited out. Rainer Schulte, editor of *Translation Review*:

> The translator is first of all also a reader, but a reader of a different kind who leaves nothing untouched in the act of reading. Every detail, every repetition of words, images, sounds, the spaces between paragraphs, the creation of new words, and other linguistic idiosyncrasies have to be registered by the translator-reader. The translator is not only concerned with 'what' is written on the page, but also 'why' it is written the way it is.

Motivations may be complex or simple, depending on the script, the genre and the character type:

Walk-ons. In and out, they are nothing more than thumbnail sketches. Background filler to give the show a sense of verisimilitude or to get the major and minor characters from one point to another. A hot dog vender, a cab driver, a bank teller. Their motivation doesn't exist except as a one-dimensional means to forward the plot. Easily recognizable stereotypes, identified more by their uniforms or service roles than as people.

Supporting. Unlike walk-ons, these characters are often fully realized. Comic relief, friends, supervisors, antagonists—essentially any speaking character that is not the main protagonist. Walk-ons sometimes have limited dialogue, but supporting characters have much more. Their motivations can be complex and difficult to discover because of their limited screen time.

Major. This may be the protagonist or the villain, but in practical terms, the more screen time a character has, the more important the role. Or the star, for that matter. Lead characters come in all sizes: hero, anti-hero, villain, altruistic, hopeful, bitter, relentless, flighty. The list goes on. But every major character in any film with lasting appeal is seeking some form of redemption. Finding it takes a bit of detective work.

Motivations come in as many shapes as the characters themselves, but they are not always obvious:

Overt. Explicitly stated by the character, or by supporting players about the protagonist. In some films this is the only motivation supplied. Unfortunately, many villains explain themselves *ad nauseum* to the hero at the end of the film. Easy to stick in subtitles because the screen time devoted to these speeches often exceeds viewer interest.

Implied. Deftly handled characters rarely explain their motives. They are often unaware of what their actions say about themselves. Their behavior speaks to their motivations, allowing viewers to infer without being bludgeoned. Notice the woman in Ed McBain's short story, "I Saw Mommy Killing Santa Claus," presented here in screenplay format. An 8-year-old boy has announced to a bookstore clerk that Santa Claus is dead. A woman waltzes down the stairs to interrupt:

> WOMAN

When I was a little girl, I saw Santa die, too.

> MAX

You did?

> WOMAN

Yes, little boy. Where do I pay for these?

> MAX

At the register. Where was this?

> WOMAN

At Macy's.

> MAX

How old were you?

> WOMAN

Never ask a woman her age. I was six.

> MAX

What happened?

> WOMAN

I was sitting on Santa's lap when he had a fatal heart attack.

ALAN

That must have been *horrible* for you.

WOMAN

Yes, I always felt I'd caused it somehow.

ALAN

But you didn't, of course.

WOMAN

Well, I'm not actually sure. I was a pretty sexy little thing,
you know. The point is, little boy, we *all* have Santas die on
us sooner or later, so I wouldn't take it too much to heart,
really. Do you gift wrap?

Observe how much the woman has revealed about herself without seem-
ing to do so. Her overt explanation of why she joins the conversation ("I
saw Santa die, too.") would seem to be motive enough, but note how her
dialogue reveals why this character type needs to bring attention to herself:

"Never ask a woman her age." She may be middle-aged,
or at least at a point where her age matters to her.

"I was a pretty sexy little thing." The line says more
about her flirtatious manner at this time in life than anything about herself at age six.

"Little boy." She's uninterested in names and people,
other than as bit players in her grand performance. She's
the type that must make an entrance and draw attention to
herself, invited or not.

"Do you gift wrap?" Having played the room, she dis-
misses it as quickly.

"We *all* have Santas die on us sooner or later." Her
closing line shows she's worldly-wise and slightly bitter.
This is quoted at the end of the short story, so its importance shouldn't be minimized.

The woman's overt explanation is not nearly as revealing as her subsequent dialogue. When creating profiles, pay attention to what the characters
say. Dialogue provides clues to help a subtitler find just the right note. Implied motivations can also be part of the current action. For example, a man
who was abducted as a child reveals his past to a rescued child, as happened
so often in *The Pretender* TV series. Flashbacks frequently serve this role.

Hidden. A character may state one motivation but be hiding another. This may be duplicitous or merely reserved. Scripts that understand natural human boundaries often have hidden motivations that are secret only because they are no one's business. Villains are all too frequently terrible liars. That is, the characters are presented as being crafty beyond words, but the actors portraying them are so shifty-eyed that the viewers are in awe at how dense the heroes must be. The better screenplays (and actors) avoid these broad interpretations. They keep hidden motivations, well, hidden.

Subconscious. Well-written television excels at subconscious motivations. Films do, as well, but TV has more time to develop psychological profiles. Often these motivations are unknown to the character and slowly come to light as part of the plot. Once identified, the subtitler must ensure the dialogue resonates with the subconscious motivations without stating them.

MacGuffins

Alfred Hitchcock popularized the term "MacGuffin" to indicate something everyone in a story wants. Character motivation drives the overall theme; a MacGuffin drives the plot. It doesn't matter what it is—an idea, an object, a chimera—as long as everyone needs it. *The Maltese Falcon* is probably the best MacGuffin in film history. Hitchcock explained:

> The theft of secret documents was the original MacGuffin. So the 'MacGuffin' is the term we use to cover all that sort of thing: to steal plans or documents, or discover a secret, it doesn't matter what it is. And the logicians are wrong in trying to figure out the truth of a MacGuffin, since it's beside the point. The only thing that that really matters is that in the picture the plans, documents, or secrets must seem to be of vital importance to the characters. To me, the narrator, they're of no importance whatever.

A MacGuffin is not motivation. It is *what* they want, not *why* they want it. Everyone in *Casablanca* wants the letters of transport; why they want them is what makes the story interesting. Another great MacGuffin is the briefcase in *Pulp Fiction*. What's in the case? Who cares? All that matters is that so many people are after it. Again, *why* they want it defines the characters and makes for intriguing cinema. The translator must know the character motivations and the MacGuffins. These plot points enter dialogue frequently and should be subtitled with care. Most films have a clearly defined goal, but episodic television has a constant need for new MacGuffins. This tradition hails back to the movie serials of the 1930s, '40s and '50s—the godfathers of modern TV. Ken Weiss and Ed Goodgold explained how serials kept renewing MacGuffins in a tongue-in-cheek description similar to *The Crimson Ghost* (1946):

The Crimson Ghost (1946)

Often we'd find the villain at a late stage in his plan to achieve his diabolical aim. All he needs is the atom-radar-cyclotizer developed by Dr. Genius. And so, for fifteen chapters, he tries to get the atom-radar-cyclotizer, and Bruce Hero, assigned to protect it, attempts to thwart him. Somewhere in the middle chapters the villain gains possession of the device and stands at the brink of success. But he inevitably discovers that the essential dyno-tube is missing. His attempts to steal the tube are good for another few chapters. Naturally, he eventually obtains the dyno-tube and stands once again on the brink of success, only to discover that he needs compound X, the special fuel required to start the damn thing. And this went on chapter after chapter, serial after serial, until our hero finally caught up with him. By the time chapter fifteen finally rolled around, both the hero and villain had very often forgotten what it was they were originally after and were enmeshed in schemes that had nothing at all to do with atom-radar-cyclotizers.

A subtitler must be aware of the constantly changing MacGuffins in television. The name of a MacGuffin will come up over and over in dialogue. Its translation must be memorable and preferably short.

Choosing Character Voices

People and the fictional characters they create have unique styles of speech. Brief or long-winded; eloquent or hesitant; literal or rhetorical. Some people revel in the form and sound of words. Others see language as a vehicle of necessary utility. Observe the clipped eloquence of the subtitles for Criterion's release of Kurosawa Akira's *The Seven Samurai* (1954):

KAMBEI

You embarrass me. You're overestimating me. . . . Listen, I'm not a man with any special skill, but I've had plenty of experience in battles; losing battles, all of them. In short, that's all I am. Drop such an idea for your own good.

KATSUSHIRO

No sir, my decision has been made. I'll follow you, sir.

KAMBEI

I forbid it. I can't afford to take a kid with me.

The Seven Samurai (1954)

Kambei, of course, is anything but a loser and the young samurai learns much by following him. Early in the film Kambei shaves his head to pose as a monk while saving a child. For the rest of the movie he rubs the bristles when distracted—a physical indicator as telling as his terse dialogue. Criterion's re-release of the film featured a new translation that retained the pacing and dignified phrasing of the Kambei character:

> I'm at a loss. You think far too highly of me. . . . Just hear me out. There's nothing special about me. I may have seen my share of battle, but always on the losing side. That about sums me up. Better not to follow such an unlucky man.

Character Indicators

Linguistic styles are not uniform within any given gender, race or background. Certainly there are similarities, but also vast differences, even among those reared in the same household, who went to the same school and had the same types of friends. With subtitles the translator's job is to identify the quirks of dialogue that indicate each character's unique speech pattern.

Most people have certain phrases they prefer, whether knowingly or not. For example, in a stressful situation, one might preface a remark with "actually..." or "now I think on it..." or any number of variations. These stall words give the speaker time to organize thoughts. Similar phrases often rear their heads in screenplays. Although the actors are reading lines and don't need stall words, screenwriters know this is one of the best ways to give a sense of natural speech to the dialogue. Writers, actors and the characters they portray all have favorite phrases, whether a simple "just" or more complete expressions, such as "the way I see it." The better programs use this to telling effect, as in David S. Ward's tight screenplay for director George Roy Hill's *The Sting* (1973):

LONNEGAN

Mr. Shaw, we usually require a tie at this table. If you don't have one, we can get you one.

GONDORFF

That'd be real nice of you, Mr. Lonniman!

LONNEGAN

Lonnegan.

Later the joke has a memorable payoff when Lonnegan loses his temper:

> The name's Lonnegan! Doyle Lonnegan! You're gonna remember that name or you're gonna get yourself a new game! Ya follow?

This scene introduces Doyle Lonnegan and his favorite pet phrase, "Ya follow?" For the rest of the film, whenever Lonnegan is threatening, "Ya follow" tags the end of the line. These tag lines are essential to many screenplays and must be translated carefully.

Dialogue indicators evolve naturally in common speech and usually occur at convenient breath points. Most well-written screenplays use indicators for colorful characters that can be replicated in the subtitles. In *Queen Seondeok*, an important character doesn't make an entrance until Episode 21, when he waltzes in fully-realized with shaggy clothes and unique speech patterns that other characters call, "His funny way of talking." There is an odd lilt to his voice at the end of most lines, almost a tonal shrug. These are not questions, per se—merely statements with a haphazard quality. To reproduce his rustic dialogue and odd phrasing, the subtitles add a "yeah" at the end of many statements, matching the smug charm of the character: "People need meat, yeah? To stay strong, yeah?" This repetition matches the character's heavy accent in the opening scenes. Later, the accent is toned down but crops up occasionally as a reminder of the young man's background. Similarly, in the subtitles, "yeah" is used in moderation for the same purpose.

Some indicators serve as humor. In Episode 42 of *East of Eden*, a humorous scene is filled with surprising pathos due to certain repetitive inflections. Dongwook stumbles in after being out all night. He has learned the identity of his real father and worries that he will no longer be accepted or loved by his family. The dialogue illustrates his brother's attitude by using informal speech patterns reserved for close family members:

DONG-CHUL

So Mr. Big Prosecutor's family is a joke to him? You stumble in after carrying on all night. Taking off without so much as a phone call? Try that again, Mr. Man, and see what happens. You understand me, mister?

DONG-WOOK

Yes.

DONG-CHUL

I didn't hear you. Speak up. You understand?

DONG-WOOK

Yes, I understand.

DONG-CHUL

Mother, Dong-wook's home.

MOTHER

What's this? Out carrying on instead of studying? This good-for-nothing says he'll study law to avenge his father, and where's he go all night? Well?

DONG-WOOK

Mother.

MOTHER

Time waits for no one, young man. Study even when you're hungry. You have to study to succeed.

DONG-WOOK

[*crying with joy*]

I'm sorry, Mom.

Repetition is a vital part of the dialogue and should be included in the subtitles. The original dialogue is filled with phrasing that would only be used by an older sibling or parent. Dong-chul's repetition of "mister" communicates to the audience his scolding tone, copying the verb endings and breath points. The mother's original dialogue has a sharp twang at the end of each sentence, a nagging inflection shown in subtitles with a question mark and her endearingly sideways sentences, so different from Dong-chul's.

Match the Style to the Character

Buffy the Vampire Slayer mines the rich depths of caricature and resonant speech styles in ways seldom seen on television. Informed with the best traditions of comic dialogue, *Buffy* pulls out all the stops: slapstick, corny buffoonery, witty wordplay, self-referential humor and slight of hand. All laced with a hint of irony. As Brian Wall and Michael Zryd point out:

> Although self-conscious and even reflexive use of irony, sarcasm and word-play on *Buffy* and *Angel* are attributable to the genre of teen comedy-drama, the use of irony and bathos function on another level to contrast the way forces of evil on both shows are given stuffy, arrogant, monumental and institutionalized form.

Buffy screenplays craft speech patterns so well that it's possible to identify characters merely by reading their dialogue. In "Buffy vs. Dracula" from Season 5, Dracula's dialogue is a formalized counterpoint to Xander's comic patter:

XANDER

You know what? You're not so big. One round of old-fashioned fisticuffs, you'd fold like a bitty baby. Okay, let's do it. And no poofing. Come on, puffy shirt. Pucker on up, cause you can kiss your pale ass—

DRACULA

Silence.

XANDER

Yes master. No, that's not—

DRACULA

You will be my emissary, my eyes and ears in daylight.

XANDER

Your emissary?

DRACULA

Serve me well. You will be rewarded. I will make you an immortal. A child of darkness that feeds on life itself... on blood.

XANDER

Blood? Yes! Yes! I will serve you, your excellent spooki-ness.

[*Dracula frowns.*]

Or master. I'll just stick with master.

DRACULA

You are strange and off-putting. Go now.

Later in the same episode, self-effacing comic dialogue about Dracula brings home the differences between the regular cast and "Count Famous":

BUFFY

I told you he'd heard of me, right? I mean, can you believe that? Count Famous heard of me.

RILEY

I couldn't believe it the first 20 times you told us, but it's starting to sink in now.

BUFFY

I'm sorry. Am I repeat-o-girl? I was just... blown away.

RILEY

It's not that surprising that he's heard of you, Buffy. You are the slayer.

BUFFY

I guess. Just—the way he said it, you know, I mean, he made it sound so...

WILLOW

Sexy? I bet he made it sound sexy.

BUFFY

Kinda. He of the dark penetrating eyes and lilty accent.

The pay-off comes near the end of the episode. Contrasting speech styles clearly delineate the two characters:

BUFFY

You think you can just waft in here with your music video wind and your hypno-eyes...

DRACULA

I have searched the world over for you. I have yearned for you. For a creature whose darkness rivals my own.

This dialogue provides lessons on creating distinct character voices.

Conjunctions. Most TV actors have great diction, but in this scene, Dracula's is exaggerated to contrast with Buffy's off-the-cuff comments. Dracula does not use a single conjunction. The *Buffy* regulars, on the other hand, take their plethora of conjunctions and toss in made-up words, like "repeat-o-girl" and "hypno-eyes". Characters who speak in slow, carefully-chosen phrases may be represented in subtitles by eliminating conjunctions entirely.

Alliteration. Note Xander's rambling challenge, filled with alliteration: "bitty baby", "poofing", "puffy", "pucker", "pale". It could be set to pop music. Dracula's serious tone is matched my clipped phrasing. Alliterative phrasing is not restricted to comic characters. It is common in many well-written screenplays and should be replicated in subtitles whenever possible. Consider this line from the final episode of *East of Eden*. Rebecca and Shin Tae-hwan had an affair. He kidnapped her and killed her baby (while still in the womb) so he could marry another woman. Rebecca switched Shin Tae-hwan's child with a miner's son in the hospital. The two boys grew up not knowing the truth about their true parents. When Shin Tae-hwan's real son, Dong-wook, learns the truth, he confronts Rebecca:

> You'd ruin the lives of others to pay for the life ripped from you.

This translation attempts to replicate the original's alliteration (ruin/ripped), repetition (lives/life) and double entendre (both the baby's life and Rebecca's own future were "ripped" from her). In the source language, a listener may pick up the dual meaning of "*saeng-sal*," a term that can mean life and death, being cut to the quick, and flesh itself—a nice reference to the overall bloodlines theme of the program. Even "*sal*" in this expression has a dual meaning of an evil spirit and bad blood in a family. This flesh/blood theme also works with the common use of the phrase, "cut like a knife."

Politeness. Formal characters lean toward perfect grammar, as do well-educated individuals. Often well-phrased grammar is seen as a type of verbal politeness. This is ideal with the Dracula persona, but should be avoided when writing subtitles for a sympathetic character. It can distance the audience from the speaker. Grammatical niceties may be observed by characters in subservient roles or those hoping to appear so. Polite phrasing may be sardonic or a thinly-veiled insult, as discussed by Peter Trudgill:

> In English the desire to convey an impression of politeness may well often lead to a greater usage of standard linguistic features, but the reverse is not true: the usage of more 'correct' language does not necessarily indicate politeness. It is perfectly possible to employ high status pronunciations and standard grammatical forms together with impolite lexis and other signals of distance and dominance.

The use of polite terms in a confrontation is illustrated in Episode 48 of *East of Eden*, when young prosecutor Dong-wook confronts the older gangster Dae-hwa. The screenplay is riddled with volatile phrases, ranging from formal to informal to demeaning. Dong-wook's dialogue is uniformly denigrating; Dae-hwa's escalates to exaggerated politeness:

DONG-WOOK

Such wisdom and refinement from a man whose tactics are so crude?

DAE-HWA

Did you say 'crude', SIR?

DONG-WOOK

Chairman Shin gets in your way, you put him in the hospital. You send your boys to rob my house.

DAE-HWA

Now hold on, SIR.

DONG-WOOK

What, MISTER?

DAE-HWA

'Mister?' I visit your little village, you call me whatever you like. But this is MY house. No one disrespects me in my own home.

The source dialogue's use of "mister" matches the same usage in English. It is often a term of respect, but can also be quite sarcastic. Dae-hwa uses an exaggerated polite verb ending and a term for a young noble (*yangban*) to remind Dong-wook of his manners. Dong-wook's reply is snide. In context, using "sir" and "mister" communicates this hostility. Later Dong-chul enters the room. Dae-hwa addresses Dong-chul, downshifting from polite forms to demeaning verbs. Although his dialogue is invidious, he is not speaking to the prosecutor, and so is free to let loose bitter invective:

DAE-HWA

And just in time. Perfect timing, in fact. Take Mr. Punk Prosecutor out of here. I can't stand his whining, I swear. He crawls in here making accusations. Maybe baby didn't get his breakfast? Lil Mr. Grumpy didn't use a single respectful term, not once. What're you waiting for? Take the baby out.

Dae-hwa belittles Dong-wook's youth and inexperience. The subtitles use terms like "punk prosecutor", "baby", "brat", and "lil Mr. Grumpy". This culminates at the end of the scene when he shouts directly at the prosecutor: "Run home and tell daddy!" By shifting from exaggerated politeness to insulting terms, the source's inventive use of verbs is displayed in the subtitles, giving the audience a sense of the scene's escalating emotions.

Dialect, Accents and Slang

Dialects can be baffling to recreate in subtitles, but not impossible. The Ray Charles quote in the first chapter is an example of how to capture dialect in written form with no loss of flavor or understanding.

The lead character in *I Really, Really Like You* has a nearly unintelligible dialect. Not merely an accent, which can be difficult enough, she speaks in a dialect that seems like a whole new language to people in Seoul. This is illustrated in simple ways, such as in Episode 16 when Bong-sun brings flowers for a little girl's "mama". The girl doesn't recognize the term, so Bong-sun must rephrase: "Ahhh… I brought these for your mother." In English, "mama" and "mother" are so similar that anyone could tell the difference, but the subtitles use the terms to show accent without being too terribly confusing. Bong-sun's dialect is represented again when she mispronounces "cabbages" as "cablages" in Episode 4. Her pronunciation is a central part of the humor in the scene:

BONG-SUN

So stop being a whiny kawt and find my money.

POLICEMAN

This is just… hang on, what's a kawt? And cablages?

BONG-SUN

What do you mean what? A kawt is a kawt. Cablages are cablages. You've never heard of a kawt? Meow, meow.

POLICEMAN

Ah, a cat. Like that old saying, 'a quiet cat catches the rat?' But what about cablages?

BONG-SUN

How can a policeman not know cablages? Don't you eat kimchi at home?

POLICEMAN

Yeah, I eat kimchi… Ah, so cablages are cabbages. So you said, 'Never count me out, I only count cabbages.' Why are country accents always such a headache?

Accents don't have to be confusing. Zane Grey's *West of the Pecos* shows how liberal use of dialect needn't stop the flow of dialogue. In this scene, reprinted in screenplay format, Pecos Smith is teaching Rill how to shoot a pistol. Note the difference in speech patterns between the characters:

PECOS

Yu have to thumb the hammer.

RILL

Shoot from the horse?

Why, shore! If yu run into a bandit would yu git off polite an' plug him from the ground?

RILL

I did meet two bandits—and I ran for all I was worth.

PECOS

Wal, yore education is beginnin'. Hold the gun high with yore thumb on the hammer. Then throw it hard with a downward jerk. The motion will flip the hammer just as the gun reaches a level, an' it'll go off, yu bet. Yu gotta sort of guess instead of aimin'.

Uniform usage. Zane Grey's use of dialect may seem unintelligible but for one important point: Grey establishes the ground rules early in each novel and never varies from them. Spelling and usage are uniform throughout. Grey's millions of fans have had no trouble understanding the characters. Indeed, his use of dialect gives the stories a unique flavor. The same is true in subtitles. Use dialect sparingly. Establish the rules of usage early and stick to them. Viewers will soon adapt to variations in spelling and infer that the character's dialogue has a unique sound that is replicated in the subtitles. When done right, the rules of usage for that specific character's dialect will barely be noticed by the viewers, so immersed will they be in the program itself. Mark Twain expands on this in his Explanatory Note preceding *The Adventures of Huckleberry Finn*:

> In this book a number of dialects are used, to wit: the Missouri negro dialect; the extremest form of the backwoods Southwestern dialect; the ordinary 'Pike County' dialect; and four modified varieties of this last. The shadings have not been done in a haphazard fashion, or by guesswork; but painstakingly, and with the trustworthy guidance and support of personal familiarity with these several forms of speech. I make this explanation for the reason that without it many readers would suppose that all these characters were trying to talk alike and not succeeding.

Matching usage to character. It is essential to know the background of a large number of expressions and match them appropriately to the character's dialogue. In Episode 37 of *East of Eden*, there is a face-off between anti-hero Dae-hwa and some Chinese assassins. Dae-hwa is complex. Studied and reserved, yet prone to explosive violence. Every line is delivered with nuance and color. He's one cool cat.

East of Eden (2009)

DAE-HWA

Who are you? What do you want?

ASSASSIN

I think you know. Who sent the hitman to Macau, you or
Lee Dong-chul?

DAE-HWA

How about you pop open the coffin and ask him, you 'tard.

The unpleasant 'tard is short for retard, an epithet for a mentally ill person. The term is unacceptable in polite society. But these characters are not
concerned with social etiquette, as is clear in the vulgar literal translation:

What the..? You really ARE a stupid son of a bitch.

However, the source phrasing barely skates around a family TV rating, so
the subtitle must use a term that's equally unsettling without being overtly
crude. Unpleasant names are frequently translated as "jerk" or "idiot."
Both terms have their place, but lack character. For an older gangster like
Dae-hwa, "punk" is the best way to express his disdain:

ASSASSIN

You have to send some bum to kill our boss? Crush him!

DAE-HWA

You really ARE a 'tard. Crush me? Am I a cookie? Crush
me? C'mon punk! C'mon and throw down!

An idiomatic expression may seem modern when it has actually been in
use for centuries. "Throw down" has come to mean issuing a challenge or
entering into a fight. The term originated with medieval knights: one would
throw down his gauntlet to demand a joust; the second would pick it up to
accept. The latter usage hails to the Old West. A Colt Single Action Army
revolver, or Peacemaker, had to be cocked after each firing. Pulling the
trigger caused the hammer to drop. To speed up the process, a gunfighter
would "throw it hard with a downward jerk," as illustrated in Zane Grey's
quintessentially western phrasing. "Throw down" is slang, but slang with
pedigree. It may be used with little worry that it will grow dated. The assassin is threatening Dae-hwa with a sword. The literal translation of a common challenge in the source language ("C'mon and stab me") sounds forced
in English. Dae-hwa's body language clearly invites the assassin to attack, so
an English equivalent was ideal, capturing the tone of the dialogue and Dae-
hwa's unique speech patterns. The middle-aged but still dangerous Dae-hwa
has doubtless used such terms many times in his criminal career.

Dae-hwa has a slight dialect, represented in subtitles with such easily-understood expressions as 'tard and c'mon. More important, he frequently uses repetition to make a point ("Crush me? Am I a cookie? Crush me?"), a dialogue indicator that is immediately recognizable throughout all 56 episodes of the series. The explosive anger of the scene, its sudden violence, is ideally suited to using a phrase that fits both older and younger characters.

Matching usage to source. A subtitler must identify the screenwriter's interpretation of an historical piece relevant to the original target audience, not the period in which the show takes place. Lord Sudley addressed this point in the introduction to his translation of *The Three Musketeers*: "In his historical romances Dumas made his characters talk as they would have talked in his own day, not as they talked in the period with which he was dealing." The tone and style of a screenplay is usually written with the current viewers in mind. For example, the attitudes toward a young couple crossing class boundaries in *The Seven Samurai* represent the views of the time in which it was filmed. They certainly do not reflect a 16th-century Japanese perspective.

This is particularly true with comic relief characters, who invariably serve their purpose with humor and asides appropriate to the audience. Most historical epics have characters whose jokes may not be topical but will invariably appeal to the viewers. The subtitler, then, has a two-fold translation challenge:

1. Create subtitles that reflect the period of the program content;
2. Create subtitles that reflect the period for which the screenplay was written.

Clare Sullivan discussed this issue in an essay on her translation of *Un martes como hoy* (2004) by Cecilia Urbina. The short novel is set in the American Old West, as related by modern Mexican characters whose speech patterns have been influenced by Hollywood westerns. Sullivan reveals how she nearly lost sight of Urbina's artistry in pursuit of period accuracy. "The initial mistake, which was rooted primarily in the dialogue, was an honest one" writes Sullivan on her translation, "springing from a translator's instinct to authentically render period language."

The parallel plots deal with a modern love triangle between the storytellers themselves and the wildly exaggerated Old West fantasy of Francisco Videgaray. For the latter plot Sullivan chose expressions completely at odds with truly period dialogue, but perfectly suited to the storytellers perceptions of the Old West, including frequently hokey clichés rooted in film. Sullivan explains the goal of this exaggerated phrasing:

It served to shed light on the deeper meanings of the novel that might not have been present had I executed either a word-for-word translation, or one that stayed 'truer' to the period speech that suffused the Francisco tale. Though I can conceive of a sense in which this might be considered bad translation (at least in the narrow sense), in the end I believe it serves the reader by inviting deeper entry into the novel.

This does not mean every period piece should be adapted to modern slang. If slang must be used, it properly belongs to the period in which the program aired. As translator John Hollander points out, ". . . probably the most satisfactory and effective translations will have the virtue of being appropriate to their literary and historical milieus." For example, John Carpenter's *Halloween* (1978) features a character who agrees with everything by exclaiming, "Totally!" It's dated, true, but a part of the film and loved by its many fans. Subtitles for *Halloween* must identify similar slang from 1978 in the target language to capture the charm of the original. Translating it to 21st-century slang would be all wrong. Yet classic films should be translated with modern viewers in mind. Richard Howard observed "it must be acknowledged that all translations date; certain works never do." Howard continued: "Time reveals all translation to be paraphrase, and it is in the longing for a standard version of a 'beloved' work that we must begin again, we translators—that we must overtake one another." It is difficult to find phrases that appeal to the current audience while honoring the original. Anthony Briggs discussed this balance in the notes to his 2005 translation of *War and Peace*:

> Language changes and, without worshiping modernity for its own sake, publishers recognize the need to accommodate new readers by using phrasing more closely attuned to their way of speaking. . . . On the other hand, it is most important not to over-modernize. Tempting though it may be, I cannot use popularized phrases like 'buzzword', 'oddball' or 'hooliganism'.

Jargon

Each film has its own unique jargon, particularly police procedurals, historical epics or medical shows. A subtitler needs reference material that matches the dialogue. The original screenwriter did the same thing; and then adapted the jargon to add a sense of verisimilitude to the program. The subtitles are yet another step removed: first the source material; second the screenwriter's adaptation; and finally the translation of the screenplay. The translator is best served by using the jargon most common in similar US programs.

Setting the Pace

Some subtitles suffer from poor timing. They are too long or too short for the on-screen audio. For many subtitle professionals, the trick isn't matching the words to the time allowed—it's giving those words the right feel for the scene so they ring true as well as fit nicely. Well-realized characters often have speech mannerisms that present unique challenges to the subtitler.

Patter & Chatter

The screenplay for Martin Scorsese's *Goodfellas* (1990) was written by Nicholas Pileggi and Scorsese, based on Pileggi's book about Henry Hill, *Wiseguy: Life in a Mafia Family*. The dialogue is rich with the flavor of the genre, as in the rationalizations of Hill's wife:

> They were blue-collar guys. The only way they could make extra money, real extra money, was to go out and cut a few corners.

Some of Hill's best lines in composite:

> As far back as I can remember, I always wanted to be a gangster. To me, being a gangster was better than being President of the United States. To me, it meant being somebody in a neighborhood that was full of nobodies. They weren't like anybody else. I mean, they did whatever they wanted. They double-parked in front of a hydrant and nobody ever gave them a ticket. In the summer when they played cards all night, nobody ever called the cops. We were treated like movie stars with muscle. Today, everything is different. There's no action. I have to wait around like everyone else.

Hill's character voice rings true. It has a cadence that carries the viewer along with the action, eliciting empathy without asking for it. Ray Liotta's performance as Henry Hill in *Goodfellas* comes fast and furious. It's entertaining: rapid-fire with just the right inflection. But it's unlikely every word could fit in the time and space available for subtitles. It's a harsh reality of the medium. Something must be lost:

> As long as I can remember I wanted to be a gangster. Being a gangster was better than being president. It meant being somebody in a neighborhood of nobodies. They weren't like anybody else. They did what they wanted. They double-parked in front of hydrants and never got a ticket. When they played cards all night, nobody called the cops. We were

treated like movie stars with muscle. Today, everything's different. There's no action. I have to wait around like everyone else.

This edit shaves the dialogue from 105 to 82 words. It also provides breath points so the subtitles flow naturally between pauses. It keeps some of the repetition ("gangster" and "they") but sacrifices other character indicators ("To me" and "I mean"). In a perfect world a subtitler would never have to change a word of such wonderful dialogue. But viewers can only read so fast. Some characters talk faster. Other films save that urgency for emergencies. In either case, a subtitler must edit rapid speech to its essentials. Some lines are screamed without pause:

The-house-next-to-us-is-on-fire-I-saw-flames-in-their-kitchen!

This can be edited to:

The neighbor's house is on fire!

Of course, every translator hates to do it. It goes against the grain. But when time is short, the decision must be made. Russian filmmaker Sergei Eisenstein's advice on montage applies to translation as well: "The task is creatively to dissect the theme into its determining representations and then to combine these representations in such a way as to call to life the *initial image of the theme*." Subtitlers do this every day.

Comic characters often fill short screen time with witty and extravagantly fast-paced patter. Editing hilariously rambling dialogue for space is heartbreaking. Most subtitlers would love to share the full, rich comedy of the original. However, audiences can be trusted. Comic characters are easy to recognize. Their frantic tone is coming through the audio track loud and clear. Viewers recognize that every word may not make it on the screen in the limited time available. Give them the best bits:

1. The set-up
2. The punchline
3. Edit the excess

Irrelevant chatter requires little sacrifice, as with most news announcers and politicians as presented in film. This dialogue sometimes has important information, but is couched in the brain-numbing rhetoric so common to the news or public speakers:

Governor Yakkalot said today in a speech in Central Park that he 'appreciates each and every contribution he received' as the election campaign scandal continues.

If the scandal is the key plot point, this type of chatter can be legitimately edited to its component parts:

The governor commented on his campaign contributions today.

If the location of the speech is important:

The governor addressed the contributions scandal in Central Park today.

News commentary has its own style that deserves full consideration in a documentary. But as expository dialogue in film, there's little time for a full translation. Subtitles need to get the point across so the main plot can move forward. Again from Rainer Schulte:

Words have their primary and secondary meanings, which makes it easier to recognize 'what' is in a text. However, like the notes of a score, words change their inherent power of communications as soon as they enter into relationships with other words, images, or metaphors. This situation should prompt the translator as reader to move from the statement of 'what' is in the text to 'why' it is there.

Slow Talkers

There are slow talkers. Very... slow. Many melodramas have funereal pacing that fills the screen with long pauses:

Revelatory. Usually some important revelation is stuck at the end of a sentence with a few pauses in-between. Consider this literal translation: "Shin Tae-hwan... your father... is." In the source language, until the character mutters the verb ("is"), the audience has no clue what relationship exists between Shin Tae-hwan and the father in question. However, in English that sentence is silly. Better to save the revelation for the end, honoring the intent of the original: "Shin Tae-hwan... is... your real father."

Sad. This type of slow dialogue has specific breath points, usually for tears, gasps or sighs. Time subtitles to match the pauses while retaining the natural pace.

Dying words. Character's last words are usually filled with pathos. They are important. In Episode 24 of *Queen Seondeok*, Princess Chungmyung is dying. Her twin sister, Deokman, is racing to find medicine. The Princess looks into the fire and softly whispers in literal translation:

Deokman... I want to see you.

The scene cuts to Deokman spurring her horse to get back. But she will be too late. The original scene is filled with a sense of tragedy and terrible longing. "Deokman... I miss you" is awful, a weak whimper. "I'll miss you" is stronger, but the dialogue is emphatically in the present tense. "Deokman... I want to see Deokman" is impersonal, as though addressing an auditorium. Viewers have stayed with this show for 24 episodes. They are likely fans of the program and more than a few will be caught up in the moment of the scene. The lines in a death scene must be weighed carefully to convey just the right note:

Deokman... where are you...

Stuttering

Characters stutter for any number of reasons: surprise, anger, hurt, shyness. Comic characters even more so. Subtitles don't have to be an exact transcription, however. The character may sputter, "Wha-wha-what-what? What are you..? What?" Usually stutters come quickly. The audience can see and hear the action. The subtitle need only communicate over which word the character is struggling:

Wh... what're you..? What?

This translation gives viewers time to focus on the stuttering character rather than the subtitle.

Disjointed

Continuing with *Queen Seondeok*, the princess' dying wish was that her twin sister, Deokman, live a normal life. Deokman verbally wrestles with her decision. Her thoughts are disjointed. The dialogue comes at right angles, turning back on itself. The big moment comes at the end of the sentence. The subtitles should reflect her convoluted speech pattern while leading to the decision at the end:

My sister's last wish. I can't do it.
I can't bring myself to it. No... I won't.

Guarded

Guarded characters are often evasive. They may be hiding something. When translating, keep in mind that only what is actually said should appear on the screen. Often subtitles are filled with meanings that the original audience would naturally infer, but must be explicitly stated in English. Fair enough. But with guarded dialogue, these implied meanings must be part of the character's speech with no hints other than what's actually in the words themselves. Remember, the viewers don't know what's coming. Subtitles should never ruin the fun.

Minimalist

A reserved character is far different from a guarded or evasive one. Minimalist dialogue can appear flat. It is extraordinarily brief. It seems to have no flavor, no panache. But it is not always boring cinema. The actors and the context of the film make it exciting. Observe screenwriter David Webb Peoples' deft touch near the end of Clint Eastwood's *Unforgiven* (1992):

> LITTLE BILL
>
> I don't deserve this, to die like this. I was building a house.
>
> WILL
>
> Deserve's got nothin' to do with it.

Much is left unsaid. But anyone who has seen the film remembers this powerful scene. Near the end of *Queen Seondeok*, Misaeng confronts his nephew, Bidam, for what he feels was misplaced trust. Misaeng and others had hoped Bidam would be king. Bidam's mother, Misil, had her own plans for him and Bidam's tutor, Munno, reared the boy to be a great leader. The tone of this dialogue is poignant, reproachful, hurt:

> MISAENG
>
> To think that you could be anything like Misil. I was such a fool. We pinned all our hopes on you. Our absurd hopes. My sister was wrong about you too.
>
> BIDAM
>
> Hopes. Born of Misil's dreams. Reared for Munno's. Weren't you just using me for yours?

What was subtitled as "hopes" here is a Korean word meaning great purpose, achievement, aspiration, righteous cause, etc. The word doesn't quite work in subtitles. Misaeng is clearly referring to their hopes/aspirations. Bidam then contrasts hopes/aspirations with dreams/goals, combining the two in his last line. The translation is most effective as "hopes and dreams." The words are short and clear; they match the pacing and overall tone. In the original, Bidam's final line is brief. Although he includes the two terms in question, they are too long for subtitles. The audience can easily infer that they are both implied in the sentence, "Weren't you just using me for yours?"

The joy of minimalist dialogue for a translator is that it's easy to stick in subtitles. It tends to be short and to the point. The challenge is to keep it as poignant as the original. Finding just the right words to match the context of minimalist dialogue takes time. It is hard work, as famously written by Blaise Pascal in 1656: "The present letter is a very long one, simply because I had no time to make it shorter."

Find the Redemption

The characters that move us seek redemption. Think of Rick's reclamation in *Casablanca*, Darth Vader's in the *Star Wars Trilogy* and Antonius Block's in *The Seventh Seal*. *Groundhog Day, Ikiru* and *Unforgiven* are so obviously about redemption it should go without saying. Redemption is the overarching theme of the *Godfather* films. Don Corleone is redeemed through loyalty; Michael is irredeemable due to the lack of it. Sam Spade in *The Maltese Falcon* is redeemed by, of all things, loyalty to a partner he didn't even like. "When a man's partner is killed," Spade says, "he's supposed to do something about it." Batman seeks redemption for asking his mother to wear the pearls that lead to her death at the hands of a mugger; he seeks to redeem the city his father loved. Even action heroes like Ripley in the *Alien* series seek redemption—first as a mother figure in *Aliens* and later by giving her life in *Alien³*. There is little doubt that *Terminator 2* is a morality play with redemption at its heart. The *Harry Potter* films, filled with such courage and self-sacrifice, are essentially about the redemption of Harry (tormented by guilt over his parents), Dumbledore (tortured by his failure with Tom Riddle), Snape, and in a way the entire wizard world. Eddie Murphy's *The Nutty Professor* is a character of hidden pathos: beneath the surface a man is seeking to be redeemed in his own eyes. Biographical films need this urgency, as explained by screenwriting teacher Michael Hauge:

> Movies can even tell life stories, but if the subject's life is not defined by a singular visible desire—winning Jenny's love in *Forest Gump*, for example—the film will likely be a disappointment at the box office.

Jenny's redemption gives the film heart. Stories of this nature resonate deeply with viewers. *Rocky* seeks redemption, as does Rambo in *First Blood*. In *Pretty Woman*, both lead characters are redeemed by love. Even in horror, the most telling characters seek to be redeemed, as in *Frankenstein* and *The Wolf Man*. It's the most popular theme in vampire films from *Dracula* to *Twilight*. Jennifer Beals, who played the same character in *The Bride* (1985), discussed the mythic quality of *The Bride of Frankenstein* (1935):

> What I've come to realize is that these movies are out myths, our modern myths. They are our way of trying to understand the passage from life to death and what happens when you pass over. . . . The movies teach us this lesson again and again. It's a lesson we never seem to learn very well, but perhaps that's part of what makes us human. After all, what could be more human about the monster than his desire for companionship, for a bride?

The Bride of Frankenstein (1935)

Not all films are about redemption, but the most memorable characters seek it. In a final scene of *East of Eden*, Rebecca reveals her need to be redeemed in a speech filled with self-loathing and hatred for Shin Tae-hwan:

> Do you even know why I hate you so much? You know what hurts worse than being cut open and losing my child? The pain of being rejected. The pain of loving a man more than life and being cast aside like I was nothing. You and I have been dwelling in the land east of Eden. The land where Cain was banished after killing Abel. That land where humanity in all its evil has lived ever since. Where your life of ego and greed made you betray everyone around you. Where my life of revenge twisted the fates of two innocent babies. We poison everything. The world is better off without us. So today I'm going to rid the world of your evil. You deserve to burn in the lowest level of hell. And I... I can't live in this ugly world any longer. . . . There's only one road to redemption left to us. And I'm taking you to hell with me.

Shortly after her speech, Rebecca kills Shin Tae-hwan and herself. There is poetry in the dialogue's harsh, bitter finality. Rebecca paraphrases the famous quotation: "And Cain went out from the presence of the LORD, and dwelt in the land of Nod, on the east of Eden." (Genesis 4:16.) *Nod* is the Hebrew root of the verb "to wander". The *East of Eden* script follows the standard interpretation that this passage means Cain was cursed to wander the land forever. Rebecca's dialogue represents this as a land where evil thrives, the land in which she and Shin Tae-hwan have chosen to live. The subtitle phrasing is appropriate to the biblical themes and will be recognizable to most English-speaking audiences.

When creating a character profile that will guide a subtitle project, first find the redemption. The character's motivations and the underlying themes of the program will then be clear.

Chapter Three

Context

GASTON

If I were your father, which fortunately I am not, and you made any attempt to handle your own business affairs, I would give you a good spanking—in a business way, of course.

MARIETTE

What would you do if you were my secretary?

GASTON

The same thing.

MARIETTE

You're hired.

—*Trouble in Paradise* (1932)

Quentin Tarantino's *Inglourious Basterds* (2009) is a subtitle oddity. Tarantino's screenplay is liberally sprinkled with directions like "They speak French, subtitled in English," but the script itself is in English. It was translated for the French, German and Italian speaking roles, with Tarantino's original English script serving as subtitles. The subtitles more accurately represent Tarantino's intent than the spoken dialogue.

Lt. Aldo Raine's opening speech is timed after viewers have seen heinous Nazi tactics at work. His monologue is a masterpiece of characterization, dialogue and rhetoric. It is also highly entertaining and instructive:

LT. ALDO

My name is Lt. Aldo Raine and I'm puttin' together a special team. And I need me eight soldiers. Eight-Jewish-American-soldiers. Now y'all might of heard rumors about the armada happening soon. Well, we'll be leavin' a little earlier. We're gonna be dropped into France, dressed as civilians. And once we're in enemy territory, as a bushwackin', guerrilla army, we're gonna be doin' one thing and one thing only—<u>Killin'</u> <u>Nazis</u>.

The members of the National Socialist Party have conquered Europe through murder, torture, intimidation, and terror. And that's exactly what we're gonna do to them. Now I don't know 'bout y'all? But I sure as hell didn't come down from the goddamn Smoky Mountains, cross five thousand miles of water, fight my way through half Sicily, and then jump out of a fuckin' air-o-plane to teach the Nazis lessons in humanity. Nazi ain't got no humanity. They're the foot soldiers of a Jew-hatin', mass murderin' maniac, and they need to be destroyed.

That's why any and every son-of-a-bitch we find wearin' a Nazi uniform, they're gonna die.

We will be cruel to the Germans, and through our cruelty, they will know who we are. They will find the evidence of our cruelty in the disemboweled, dismembered, and disfigured bodies of their brothers we leave behind us. And the Germans will not be able to help themselves from imagining the cruelty their brothers endured at our hands, and our bootheels, and the edge of our knives.

And the Germans will be sickened by us.

And the Germans will talk about us.

And the Germans will fear us.

And when the Germans close their eyes at night and their subconscious tortures them for the evil they've done, it will be thoughts of us that it tortures them with.

Sound good?

ALL

Yes, sir!

That's what I like to hear. But I got a word of warning to all would-be warriors. When you join my command, you take on a debit. A debit you owe me, personally. Every man under my command owes me one hundred Nazi scalps. And I want my scalps. And all y'all will git me one hundred Nazi scalps, taken from the heads of one hundred dead Nazis... or you will die trying.

A subtitler must understand the nature of good dialogue in the source language and the target language. Raine's highly entertaining speech is much more than it appears on the surface. Study the character's phrasing in the source material. Learn what he says to others and what that says about Raine:

Characterization. At first reading, the Raine character seems to be nothing more than what he pretends—a particularly erudite hillbilly. But beneath his stereotypical histrionics is a cunning and talented leader of men. From this speech the audience immediately intuits Raine's inherent charm and persuasiveness. His use of propaganda techniques and rhetoric does not make him a hypocrite. The methods he uses to convince, inspire and lead are not deceitful. The character inspires loyalty by ably communicating his intent in the most colorful and exacting terms.

Dialogue. Note the judicious use of repetition throughout. Were this translated and the subtitler succumbed to the editorial temptation to remove repetition, the persuasive power of this speech would be significantly hindered. The speech has a cadence and rhythm that deserves careful study. It matches Raine's accent. Even the cursing is well-timed, lending a sense of verisimilitude. Consider the progression of his repetition, first from the word Jew to Nazi, segueing into the word cruel, and ultimately encompassing all of the evils he describes in the main enemy: the Germans. He describes what the Germans will imagine, just as the Jews listening to his speech may envision of their own brothers. His alliteration ("disemboweled, dismembered, and disfigured") is also telling.

Rhetoric. Observe how Raine first challenges the men with a harsh and thankless task, lacing his speech with frequent references to their Jewish heritage. He inspires them to rise to this challenge, infuriates them with descriptions of atrocities enacted on their people, and demonizes the Nazis by typifying them as non-human. Then he invites the men to participate in something larger than themselves, something worthwhile, something that needs doing. Now that the men have been given personal and patriotic reasons to risk their lives, Raine takes it a step further and commits them to pledges of loyalty to himself, their leader in the endeavor.

Context. Tarantino's screenplay is not merely an exercise in one-dimensional propaganda. No, Raine's character proves worthy of loyalty. His rhetoric represents his own deeply-held beliefs. This moving dialogue is summed up in a simple requirement. The men are given something tangible they can do to fulfill Raine's request and act according to their own desires: get those scalps. This sets the stage for the rest of the film. The audience infers much of the Raine character and the role the Basterds will play in the plot. The speech would be a rambling monologue in any other context. But in this film it as good as screenplays get.

Discover the rich speech patterns of the screenplay and attempt to replicate them as best possible in the subtitles. To do this, it is important to understand the context of the dialogue within individual scenes and the overall film.

Understanding Context

Context often gives dialogue great weight. Identify the style of the film: noir, comedy, historical epic, drama, melodrama, action, thriller. Sub-categorize further: teen comedy, romantic comedy, sex comedy, gross-out comedy, mismatched identity, fish-out-of-water. A subtitler must be clear on the style of dialogue used in the film. It informs each scene and the program as a whole.

Find the Subtext

Every scene has a point. Characters are learning, revealing, seeking. They find something entirely different from what they intended. They discover nothing but keep trying. They discuss what they have learned, leading to a decision. They may never mention what that something is. Or say one thing and seek another. The script holds clues, as explained by Kate Wright:

> If actions speak louder than words, then dialogue does not—and cannot—tell a story. Dramatic conflict, unconscious conflict, and dramatic subtext are revealed as inner workings of the emotional story. Dialogue, however, is only a representation of what a character says, reflecting these deeper meanings. Although dialogue is considered important to great screenwriting, less is more. Using dialogue to expose the story—expository dialogue—is a trap. It seems easy. It seems seductive. It brings the story to a halt because it is dreadful to watch.

If the characters do not say it, neither should the subtitles. But the translator must understand the subtext of the dialogue. The characters have expectations, desires, quirky habits, friends, families and enemies. Identify the point of each scene and let that subtext inform the subtitles.

Past, Present and Future

No scene exists in a vacuum. The subtitler may have started translating the third act before morning coffee, but the viewer did not. Keep the dialogue fresh and active. Each scene has a past, present and future.

The Past. What was on screen immediately prior to the current scene. More often than not it has little bearing on the characters themselves, but for the audience the timing can impact how the dialogue is perceived. In the example from *Inglourious Basterds*, the audience watched a brilliant and disgusting Nazi slaughter a Jewish family just prior to Raine's speech. The viewers empathize with Raine's men. The scene is paced and filmed for just this effect. Characters' backgrounds are also part of the past. Any earlier scenes involving the characters must be considered, as well as anything other characters have said about them. This includes off-screen action.

The Present. The current scene. Better screenplays are load-bearing. The lines say as much about character as plot.

The Future. As with the past, the future is important thematically. The scene will lead to another, often unrelated to the characters currently on-screen. The dialogue may refer to another player in the drama that then appears. Sometimes there seems to be no relation at all, except in the overall context of the film. A tender scene may be juxtaposed against a violent one, for example, or a slapstick moment followed by introspection to give the audience time to recover. The characters' futures in the screenplay must be considered. Think about how the dialogue will affect the plot and the future, both in individual scenes and throughout the film.

Roles & Relationships

Roles. People play roles, often behaving in stereotypical ways to fulfill their images of how things should be. An aging stripper adapts the refined tone she associates with her new role as grandmother. An overbearing father is subservient to his boss. Robert Brock Le Page and Andrée Tabouret-Keller:

> . . . *all* utterances are affected by the audience, the topic and the setting. . . the individual creates for himself the patterns of his linguistic behaviour so as to resemble those of the group or groups with which from time to time he wishes to be identified, or so as to be unlike those from whom he wishes to be distinguished.

The quote that began this chapter is from a classic comedy of roles, *Trouble in Paradise*. Roles might be sincere or manipulative. Perhaps they are subconscious: a desire to behave in a way expected by others or to convince oneself of a role that may or may not reflect reality. Understanding these roles gives subtitles depth.

Trouble in Paradise (1932)

Relationships. Answer these questions and the context becomes clear:

Who's related to whom? How are they related?
How do they know each other? How do they feel about each other?
How does the dialogue reflect and change this relationship?

Once the subtitler has identified the relationships, it's easier to find the right tone. Even an innocuous "What times is it?" may be phrased differently depending on the context of the scene and the characters in question. The phrasing tells much about their roles:

Polite: Do you know the time?/May I ask the time?
Informal: What time do you have?/Got the time?
Sideways/Comic: What's your watch say?/Got a watch?

Only one of these will do. The translator's craft identifies which is accurate. The subtitler's art discovers which is perfect.

Humor

Brilliant comedies don't have a lot of jokes. The humor is contextual. It would take a week to explain why a scene is funny, and even then the listener wouldn't truly understand the wit that led to a particular zinger. Mark Twain explained:

> The humorous story depends for its effect upon the *manner* of the telling; the comic story and the witty story upon the *matter* . . . The humorous story may be spun out to great length, and may wander around as much as it pleases, and arrive nowhere in particular; but the comic and witty stories must be brief and end with a point. The humorous story bubbles gently along, the others burst. The humorous story is strictly a work of art—high and delicate art—and only an artist can tell it; but no art is necessary in telling the comic and the witty story; anybody can do it . . . The humorous story is told gravely; the teller does his best to conceal the fact that he even dimly suspects that there is anything funny about it; but the teller of the comic story tells you beforehand that it is one of the funniest things he has ever heard, then tells it with eager delight, and is the first person to laugh when he gets through. . . . And when he prints it, in England, France, Germany, and Italy, he italicizes it, puts some whooping exclamation points after it, and sometimes explains it in a parenthesis. All of which is very depressing, and makes one want to renounce joking and lead a better life.

Jokes abound. They can be entertaining in themselves, but the joke's context within the humor of the screenplay is what truly gets the laughs. The gags are situational and depend on the fictional world created by the script and the viewer's knowledge of expectations in the real world, as explained by Ashley Brown and John Kimmey: "The essence of a comic situation, high or low, is incongruity: the contradiction between an individual's actions and the laws or principles which we think he should observe . . . Most of the time we see men and women whose fixed behavior makes them ridiculous only in relation to some social norm." This incongruity is especially apparent in comic asides.

Comic asides. Typically half-muttered throw-away lines, asides can be notoriously difficult to translate. An employee gets a raise from a grumpy boss. "Better get out of here before he changes his mind," he says and bolts for the door. A preening hero brags on a new hairdo. The perky sidekick mumbles, "Oh yeah, you're gorgeous... *not.*" The aside has two goals: to say what the character really thinks (and what everyone would say if they dared); and to be funny. Asides are fast. The subtitle must be brief and charming. Find the right tone within the context of the scene. The aside is more endearing than snide. It invites the viewers to the side of the speaker.

Consider the context of this exchange from *My Wife is a Superwoman*. Ji-ae, once a popular teen, is now something of a frump. Throughout the program she frequently imagines what she might say, if she dared, via fantasies enacted on screen. In Episode 6 she is being dressed down by her mother-in-law, but Ji-ae's behavior is still influenced by her old role as the prettiest girl in school. This incongruity provides the underlying humor.

MOTHER-IN-LAW

In my day, I was MUCH prettier than you ever were. They said I could have been Miss Korea. But I couldn't be bothered with beauty salons. It was my place to stand behind my husband the last 30 years. But you? You make your husband be a driver!

JI-AE

Aren't you being a little hard on me? Who supported him for the seven years he's been out of work? You think that food just appeared out of nowhere? I'd like to dress nice and go shopping and learn yoga. You wouldn't judge me if you really knew how things are. Oh, and I've seen your wedding photos. You're no Miss Korea. If Miss Korea heard that she'd be furious. [*To herself*] Did I say that out loud? I couldn't have. I imagined it—

You nuts?

JI-AE

[*To herself*] I did! I said it out loud!

The joke, of course, is in Ji-ae finally speaking out loud what she usually would only fantasize. But the *humor* is in the context and the bantering tone of the protagonists. There may be outright laughs in a given scene, but rarely does a one-off gag have the staying power of a truly humorous program. In Neil Simon's play, *The Sunshine Boys*, the jokes are funny but the pleasure of this scene is the unique relationship between theatrical agent Ben and his Uncle Willie, an old vaudeville great:

BEN

I've submitted you twenty times.

WILLIE

What's the matter with twenty one?

BEN

Because the word is out in the business that you can't remember the lines and they're simply not interested.

WILLIE

[*That hurt.*] I couldn't remember the lines? COULDN'T REMEMBER THE LINES? I don't remember that.

BEN

For the Frito-Lays potato chips. I sent you over to the studio, you couldn't even remember the address.

WILLIE

Don't tell me I didn't remember the lines. The lines I remembered beautifully. The name of the potato chip I couldn't remember... What was it?

BEN

Frito-Lays.

WILLIE

Say it again.

BEN

Frito-Lays.

WILLIE

I still can't remember it... Because it's not funny. If it's funny, I remember it. Alka-Seltzer is funny. You say 'Alka-Seltzer,' you get a laugh... the other word is *not* funny. What is it?

BEN

Frito-Lays.

WILLIE

Maybe in *Mexico* that's funny, not here... Fifty-seven years I'm in this business, you learn a few things. You know what makes an audience laugh. Do you know which words are funny and which words are not funny?

BEN

You told me a hundred times, Uncle Willie. Words with a 'K' in it are funny.

WILLIE

Words with a 'K' in it are funny. You didn't know that, did you? If it doesn't have a "K" it's not funny... I'll tell you which words always get a laugh. [*About to count on fingers.*]

BEN

Chicken.

WILLIE

Chicken is funny.

BEN

Pickle.

WILLIE

Pickle is funny.

BEN

Cup cake.

WILLIE

Cup cake is funny... Tomato is *not* funny. Roast beef is *not* funny.

BEN

But cookie is funny.

WILLIE

But cookie is funny.

BEN

Uncle Willie, you've explained that to me ever since I was a little boy.

WILLIE

Cucumber is funny.

BEN

[*Falling in again.*] Car keys.

WILLIE

Car keys is funny.

BEN

Cleveland.

WILLIE

Cleveland is funny... Maryland is *not* funny.

Willie's speech has rhythm and grace earned through years on the stage. He falls into the routine like greeting an old friend. The repetition and alliteration are all part of the jokes—and they *are* funny—but it is the underlying tone of tragedy and warmth that gives the scene its gentle humor. Focus on humor rather than jokes. Inform the subtitles with the same charm.

Stress Points

A character's intent can be represented by adding stress points to the subtitles. Consider how each stress point alters tone:

Worried: MUST you go?
Confrontational: Must YOU go?
Frantic: Must you GO?

Reality

Avoid pedestrian subtitles. They should be realistic, certainly, but only within the reality created by the screenplay. It is a fictional world, one that plays by its own rules. Dialogue from *Alien* is far different from that in *The Godfather* or *M*A*S*H*. Using subtitles that sound as though people were chatting at the local coffee ship is a disservice to the original and makes for dull viewing. Subtitles should reflect how people talk, yes—how they talk in context.

Trust the Context

Dialogue doesn't stand alone. It is part of a much larger picture. The audience has enjoyed earlier scenes and followed the characters through their troubles. Some phrasing may seem awkward, but within the film the words are deeply felt. Subtitles must not bow to breezy idioms or unsuitable colloquialisms. They should carry the same weight as the original, however melodramatic.

There is a speech near the end of *Damo* (2003) by the anti-hero Seong-baek. Out of context it seems overwrought and a little stiff. Too formal. But the scene comes after hours of viewing. It is informed by the suffering of this flawed but noble character. The dialogue is heard in voice-over during an exciting chase on horseback that may end in death. The original is intentionally melodramatic. They rush toward a cliff:

SE-UK

Turn around! Seong-baek! It's over. You took a road that's not a road.

SEONG-BAEK

'A road that's not a road.' But how is any road created? If one person walks a path… two people… if many people walk that path, it becomes a road. My only fault was trying to blaze a trail in this corrupt world.

"Blaze a trail" is a common expression to indicate creating something new. Building from a trail to a path to a road is the thematic device of the script; the translation uses the phrase to capture that intent. Seong-baek blazed a trail that will be walked by others, ". . . until at last we forge a new road, a new world." "Blaze" represents the first step of creation; "forge" the molding of something permanent, a natural progression. This scene, in this context, requires an impassioned, slightly poetic style. Anything less would seem flippant—and Seong-baek is anything but glib.

Melodrama

In the age of irony, it's easy to sneer at big emotions. Powerful, over-the-top feelings are dismissed as sham. The best films know better.

Melodrama is a part of life. People feel deeply, express themselves poorly or eloquently, are motivated and stirred by emotions that deserve a large canvas: hate, love, joy, need, ache, passion, redemption, guilt, loss, discovery. These make for great cinema. Do not avoid melodrama. Good stories are not about the mundane feelings of every day life. Write subtitles that are true to the emotional impact of the original.

The last few minutes of José Ferrer's brilliant performance in Michael Gordon's *Cyrano de Bergerac* (1950) are filled with melodrama. At the end of his life, Cyrano fancies himself surrounded by old enemies:

> All my laurels you have driven away... and my roses; yet in spite of you there is one crown I bear away with me. And tonight, when I enter before God, my salute shall sweep away all the stars from the blue threshold! One thing without stain, unspotted from the world in spite of doom mine own...
> [*raises his hand high*] and that is... my white plume.

This is a moment of depth and power. It won Ferrer a Golden Globe® and the Oscar® for Best Actor. The scene *is* melodramatic. The script is rich with emotions and isn't shy about expressing them. It dares to dream. If screenwriters Brian Hooker and Carl Foreman had feared melodrama, the film would be a tawdry farce. Compare Gladys Thomas' 1898 translation of Edmund Rostand's original play:

CYRANO

You strip from me the laurel and the rose! Take all! Despite you there is yet one thing I hold against you all, and when, to-night, I enter Christ's fair courts, and, lowly bowed, sweep with doffed casque the heavens' threshold blue, one thing is left, that, void of stain or smutch, I bear away despite you.

ROXANE

'Tis?...

CYRANO

MY PANACHE.

Hooker and Foreman understood the dramatic themes and characterization of the original. They honored the context. Carol Clark went further, using modern American English infused with melodrama but bereft of archaic terms:

CYRANO

Yes, you can take it all: the poet's crown,
The lover's garland, yet there's something still
That will be always mine, and when today
I go into God's presence, there I'll doff it
And sweep the heavenly pavement with a gesture—
Something I'll take unstained out of this world
In spite of you...

Cyrano de Bergerac (1950)

ROXANE

What, dearest?

CYRANO

My panache.

Anthony Burgess found just the right note in his translation of Jean-Paul Rappeneau's elegant French version of *Cyrano de Bergerac* (1990), written by Rappeneau and Jean-Claude Carrière. Burgess kept within the time and space constraints of subtitles while informing the dialogue with lush melodrama:

> And tonight when I, at last, God behold, my salute will
> sweep his blue threshold with something spotless.
> A diamond in the ash which I take in spite of you; and that
> is my panache.

This film won the Best Foreign Film Golden Globe® and five Oscar® nominations. The subtitles are precise, lyrical, passionate and do not insult the audience. There are few scenes in cinema as dramatic as Cyrano's death. The context in that particular film lives in the memories of many film lovers. Imagine *Persona, Rashômon, Gone With the Wind* or *Star Wars* devoid of melodrama. They'd barely be worth watching. Embrace the big emotions of the screenplay. They deserve the best a subtitler can give.

Duality & Juxtaposition

Characters say one thing and mean another. They are duplicitous. They often feel two opposing emotions at the same time. Other characters in the same scene are polar opposites—or seem to be. Juxtaposition is one of the most powerful plot devices in film. For the translator, matching the context and tone of the dialogue requires understanding the opposites in play.

Lies. Sadly, many actors portray characters that lie badly. Anyone can tell they're lying. For example, in Disney's *Scarecrow of Romney Marsh* (1963), each time the villain lays a trap for the hero he smirks, mugs at the screen, shifts his eyes right-to-left and says something like: "Why, yes, I'll meet you at midnight." Audiences groan, either because they can't believe the other characters don't see the lie, or because they're insulted that an actor doesn't lie well, the way real tricksters do. This happens in subtitles as well. In the context of the scene, the character is a good liar, the deceit is subtle and no one suspects. But the translator, spotting the lie, inserts dialogue that reveals more than the original. Avoid this. If the character is lying well, the subtitles must give nothing away.

Internal conflict. Many characters seek something. They behave at odds with their desires. This yearning leads to internal conflict. The better drinking scenes, for example, are played by actors that understand drunks don't *act* drunk. They are drunk but trying to act sober. In this juxtaposition rests the humor and the tragedy. Other characters battle their insecurities by overcompensation, as in Episode 26 of *Queen Seondeok*. The comic villain Misaeng is forever trying to impress his sister, Misil—the true villain of the program. Misaeng tries to talk tough. He isn't. He's a coward that wants others to think him brave. For example, everyone is scared of a mysterious organization of rebels called the Bokya. Misaeng plays the tough guy for his sister. Here is the literal translation:

> Those Bokya have really caused a mess. Sister, shouldn't
> we strike at the Bokya?

This subtitle fails to illustrate the comic nuances of Misaeng's dialogue and the character's blatant overcompensation. The translation should sound as tough as Misaeng is *trying* to be while retaining a sense of his histrionics:

> Those Bokya boys give me a pain. Misil, what say we give
> 'em what for?

Tough guys "give 'em what for". In *Inglourious Basterds*, Aldo Raine describes Wicki to a Nazi:

> Wicki there, an Austrian Jew, got the fuck outta Salzberg
> while the gettin' was good. Became American, got drafted,
> and came back to give y'all what for.

Misaeng is the type that affects similar dialogue to appear macho. The posturing reflects his internal conflict.

Denial. Denying accusations from others is a form of external conflict. Internal denial is powerful in the right context and deserves subtitles that understand the nature of this common human trait. In Episode 48 of *East of Eden* Young-ran confronts her dying father. Her dialogue covers the first two stages of grief:

> Why? Why are you doing this? There's too much I need to
> pay you back for. We've got things to work out, things to
> argue about! You've got to live. Ten years, at least. If not
> ten, we'll settle at three. Don't leave me. Get up now!

She's angry; then in denial. The tone and style is at first defensive and aggressive. "There's too much I need to pay you back for. We've got things to work out, things to argue about!" She shifts to denial, negotiating: "You've got to live. Ten years, at least. If not ten, we'll settle at three." The context is absolutely clear. Understanding it leads to solid subtitle choices.

Opposing characters.   Classic protagonist/antagonist oppositions are relatively simple to translate on screen.   The dialogue is often straightforward, even when snide or insinuating.   Subtle oppositions create greater challenges.   Shirley Jackson's *The Haunting of Hill House* is an example of how to hit the right note in internal and external conflicts.   Eleanor's character is steady, apologetic and careful.   She's shy, and like many shy characters, wishes she were otherwise.   She imagines herself brave, resourceful, uninhibited.   Theodora is all of the latter, yet at the same time controlling and overbearing.   Both characters are plagued by relentless self-doubt and insecurities.   Early in the novel, the dialogue effortlessly identifies the differences between the characters and what they have in common— playful natures and an eagerness to please and be accepted.   Their natures are clearly defined:

ELEANOR

Still hard to believe you're really here?

THEODORA

I had no idea it would be so dull.

ELEANOR

We'll find plenty to do in the morning.

THEODORA

At home there would be people around, and lots of talking and laughing and lights and excitement—

ELEANOR

I suppose I don't need such things.   There never was much excitement for me.   I had to stay with Mother, of course. And when she was asleep I kind of got used to playing solitaire or listening to the radio.   I never could bear to read in the evenings because I had to read aloud to her for two hours every afternoon.   Love stories—

THEODORA

I'm terrible, aren't I?   I sit here and grouch because there's nothing to amuse me; I'm very selfish.   Tell me how horrible I am.

ELEANOR

You're horrible.

The Haunting (1963)

THEODORA

I am horrible. I'm horrible and beastly and no one can stand me. There. Now tell me about yourself.

ELEANOR

I'm horrible and beastly and no one can stand me.

THEODORA

Don't make fun of me. You're sweet and pleasant and everyone likes you very much; Luke has fallen madly in love with you, and I am jealous. Now I want to know more about you. Did you really take care of your mother for many years?

ELEANOR

Yes. Eleven years, until she died three months ago.

THEODORA

Were you sorry when she died? Should I say how sorry *I* am?

ELEANOR

No. She wasn't very happy.

THEODORA

And neither were you?

ELEANOR

And neither was I.

The dialogue seems to meander, but on close examination, each character is discovering the strengths and weaknesses of the other. Theodora must control those around her. Her insecurities demand she be the center of attention and her dialogue is informed by this need, even when she seems to focus on Eleanor. In juxtaposition to Theodora's desperation, Eleanor attempts to master her insecurities by being self-contained, controlling her emotions and letting the world take care of itself.

Duality. Many films thrive on themes of duality: the lines between good and evil, right and wrong, and how easily they can become blurred. This internal struggle was best expressed by Goethe in *Faust*: "Two souls, alas, are dwelling in my breast, and one is striving to forsake its brother." Cultural historian and film critic Leo Braudy comments on how this theme intrigues audiences:

The appeal of the theme of the double, whether the doubling is within a person or projected into two characters, is to our sense of the split within, between emotions and intellect, private desires and public moral imperatives. As in *The Wolf Man*, we are torn between a loathing for it and a desire that it assume its rightful inheritance.

The title of *Time Between Dog & Wolf* comes from a common but enigmatic French expression: *L'heure entre chien et loup*, which translates literally as "The hour between dog and wolf." It is the heart of the program. Like any title, it must be thoroughly understood by the subtitler before beginning the project. Jean Genet explained the phrase:

> . . . the expression *entre chien et loup* [literally, between dog and wolf, that is, dusk, when the two can't be distinguished from each other] suggests a lot of other things besides the time of day. The colour grey, for instance, and the hour when night approaches as inexorably as sleep, whether daily or eternal. The hour when street lamps are lit in the city, and which children try to drag out so that they can go on playing, though their eyes, suddenly active, are closing in spite of themselves. The hour in which—and it's a space rather than a time—every being becomes his own shadow, and thus something other than himself. The hour of metamorphoses, when people half hope, half fear that a dog will become a wolf.

Duality is the primary theme of the drama. How each character approaches this theme is clear in the dialogue and must be convincingly subtitled. In Episode 2, Minki tries to impress a girl. Standing in front of a French painting entitled, "L'heure entre chien et loup," he waxes poetic. He comes off as a dork, but the audience sees duality unfolding despite his posturing:

> Ah yes, 'The Time between Dog and Wolf'. I haven't seen this piece since its New York exhibition two years ago. I particularly recall how the title suits the painting perfectly.
> At twilight the world burns red.
> There, a shadow creeps down the hill.
> Is it a friendly dog? Or a vicious wolf?
> In the red gloaming I cannot tell...
> *L'heure entre chien et loup.*

Minki quotes the French, lingering on the words. Gloaming is a good fit to communicate the somewhat affected nature of the character's dialogue as he holds forth in front of a pretty girl. Compare similar dialogue used by the program's hero, Kay, in a voice-over at the end of the last episode:

> At twilight the world burns red.
> A shadow creeps down the hill.
> A friendly dog? A vicious wolf?
> At this hour we can't tell.
> When good and evil blend into red.
> The time between dog and wolf.

Time Between Dog & Wolf is a classic bait and switch thriller in which no one in the audience or the program can keep up with who's doing what to whom. A subtitler must master the themes of the screenplay. A thorough understanding beyond what's on-screen is essential to finding the right tone. The poetic dialogue may seem similar but the nuances of inflection and context are slightly altered. That difference defines good subtitles.

Equivalents

A subtitler must first understand the context of a given phrase, its colloquial allusion and usage; and then find an equivalent that matches the original. This takes work. In an episode of *East of Eden*, a man wanders into the scene and is greeted by one of the shows toughest anti-heroes:

> Well, got turned into a human after all.

What? The dialogue alludes to an old proverb, literally translated as: "Speak of a tiger and it will come, losing its chance to become a noble." This proverb refers to the Korean foundation myth of a bear and tiger wanting to become human. Both are required by the son of heaven to stay in a cave for 100 days eating only garlic and mugwort. The tiger can't stand it and leaves early; the bear endures and is transformed into a woman. She unites with the son of heaven and gives birth to the founder of Korea, Tangun. Now combine the last part of the proverb, "become a noble," with another common expression, "Well, look at this," and the result is "Well, got turned into a human after all" when seeing the "tiger" under discussion wander in as a human. That little joke makes no sense outside of the foundation myth context. It's an easy English equivalent to translate this as "speak of the devil." This maintains intent but fails to give a sense of the skewering "become a noble" jibe. An alternative:

> If it isn't Mr. High-n-Mighty himself.

The sarcastic twist of "high-n-mighty" clearly implies that the person is not so lofty, just as the tiger is not a noble in the original expression. This honors the proverb and retains its colloquial flavor. Equivalents play a key role in understanding the context and characters of a program. Finding the right one requires effort and tough choices. They must not be overused and should not be an easy way out, as explained by translator John Jensen:

> My first inclination in dealing with images and metaphors is to try to use a (nearly) literal translation, but it must transmit the meaning intended by the author and not lead the text too far from its required naturalness. I fully recognize that to rely on the 'trite' and true from the native target-language stock of idioms, metaphors, and images could fail utterly to maintain the original work's voice, texture, and creativity. The role of the translator in the historical enrichment of the world's languages is tremendous. Thousands of expressions pass linguistic and culture barriers constantly through the literal translation of metaphors and calquing of idioms (think biblical translation). As purveyors of such enrichment, we must be careful in deciding what actually 'works' while respecting both languages and cultures.

Equivalents aren't always necessary. Often subtle phrasing serves the same purpose, as with this line from Episode 49 of *East of Eden*:

> You know what they say, when the tiger's away, the fox will play. And if the tiger's dead, that lil fox can't help but think he's king.

The usual equivalent is "When the cat's away, the mice will play". However, the couplet, "When the ____'s away, the _____ will play," can be adapted to the original script's animals with no loss of understanding. Viewers will recognize the formula and infer the meaning. Judicious mixing of equivalents and original intent goes a long way, as in Episode 48 of *East of Eden*:

DONG-WOOK

Everyone has dirty laundry. Don't think we won't find yours.

DONG-CHUL

So the famous prosecutor will grind my bones to dust. That what you're saying?

DONG-WOOK

If you're clean, we can avoid bloodshed.

Timing is a real problem with this scene. The brothers are angry and the dialogue comes fast. Dong-wook's first line is probably best translated as "Dust rises from everybody when they're thrashed," but that's long and awkward. "Every closet has a skeleton" or "Everyone has faults" are accurate, but a little stiff and don't fit Dong-wook's aggressive phrasing. Dong-wook is making a veiled threat: "I know you're not as clean as you pretend to be and I'll find your dirty laundry." These subtitles use crisper, briefer dialogue. Later in the scene, the translation uses the term "clean" to match "dirty laundry." Dong-chul's response, on the other hand, needs no English equivalent. "Grind my bones to dust" is clear. Equally, no equivalent is necessary for Dong-wook's rebuttal to "bones" since "bloodshed" is commonly used in confrontational dialogue.

Bridging Cultures

We are all different. And all the same. We share basic human experiences. Fathers worry about their children's safety; mothers fret on rainy days; couples plan for their futures; children rebel and come to respect their parents after all. It is how each culture deals with these and many other common human experiences that can be different. The translator must identify unique linguistic expressions that represent cultural values and, in doing so, find ways to share those differences in English. At times equivalents may be essential to communicating the full feel of a scene, as explained by linguist Dong Gu Ming:

> In the past half century, conceptual inquiries into translation have shifted from the notion of translation as a linguistic act of faithful rendition of a text from one language into another to the view of translation as an interpretive and negotiative act that privileges the target-language inscription in the foreign text and emphasizes cross-cultural representation of creative values.

"Cross-cultural representation of creative values" is a noble goal and extraordinarily difficult to achieve. On good days, when the equivalents match the context of the scene, it's worth the effort. Consider Episode 47 of *East of Eden*. Gangster Guk Dae-hwa's dialogue is always a tad off-center. He talks at angles to his intent. In this scene, his worst enemy's right-hand man has come to sell information. Dae-hwa's tone is demeaning:

DAE-HWA

Shin Tae-hwan's doggy comes sniffing round. Live long enough, you see everything. Sit, doggy.

DIRT BAG

You have what we discussed?

DAE-HWA

Give it to him. That's hot off the press. You've sniffed your money, doggy. Now speak. Let's hear what you've got, or we'll replace that attaché with a coffin. Take my meaning?

DIRT BAG

Of course, sir.

DAE-HWA

Speak, doggy.

If the source expression is vital to the plot, it must be translated literally or at least with the original allusion. However, in this scene, nothing is lost with the equivalents. They match the characters. The mood is strengthened by them.

"Doggy." This term honors the original context and the specific tone of the scene. The phrase is repeated throughout the drama by Dae-hwa and his opposite number, Shin Tae-hwan. They both have good doggies and bad and refer to them as such. Although this particular exchange did not use the term, it matches the overall context of the program. It is an equivalent that replicates Dae-hwa's disdain. The subtitles use the terms "doggy" and "sniff" to be completely demeaning. The dismissive command to sit is especially effective, since "Sit, doggy" is common worldwide. Literally, the "sniffed your money" line could have been, "You got a whiff of the money, now show me your cards," but in English, dogs are told to "speak." The "sniff" and "speak" commands work well with this metaphor. Similarly, Dae-hwa says, "Well, tell me," but to replicate the source's insulting tone and continue the metaphor, the subtitles use "Speak, doggy."

"That's hot off the press." This is the English equivalent of a common Korean phrase, "Hot from the oven." Regarding money, switching "press" for "oven" maintains the intent of the original without interrupting the flow of dialogue by inserting unnecessarily awkward phrasing.

"Attaché-coffin." Paulownia wood was traditionally used for coffins in Korea, but the term is too long for the clipped, dangerous tone in subtitles. Here the type of wood is left out but the meaning remains clear: Dae-hwa expects something for his money. Also, a soft leather bag is a "brief case" and a hard case is an attaché. A man like Guk Dae-hwa would definitely know the difference. Where another character might call it a case or a bag, Dae-hwa's use of the correct term seems even more threatening.

Proverbs, Idioms & English Equivalents

In the rich tapestry of language, nothing is as colorful as proverbs. Often humorous and filled with pathos, proverbs represent centuries-old wisdom and offer insight into a nation's history and culture. But what is understood in the source dialogue may be jarring in the target language. Revenge is a common theme in proverbs, as when the tough mob boss in *East of Eden* mutters:

> Pay me a peck and I repay a bushel.

In the source language this is a potent threat. The line is clearly a reference to the common expression, "Give a pick and get a bushel," and is an exact equivalent to the English phrase, "Sow the wind and reap the whirlwind." However, pecks and bushels aren't usually associated with angry gangsters. The English equivalent is more commonly associated with vengeance:

> Sow the wind with me and I'll repay a whirlwind.

This phrase adapts the English equivalent to capture the speaker's cold, controlled and terrifying tone. Also, the original dialogue plays on words ("give/get" becomes "pay/repay"). To replicate this, the subtitles change "reap the whirlwind" to "repay a whirlwind".

Proverbs are often filled with allusions, asides and references to the scatological, as with this well-known Korean saying: "A dog covered in dung fusses because another dog is dirty." This literal translation doesn't quite communicate the quarrelsome, bandying tone of the original. The dung reference stops the subtitles dead. If the original is essential to the plot, keep it. However, if the proverb is merely used as a common expression, it may be replaced with an exact English equivalent minus the aromatic association: "Talk about the pot calling the kettle black." It is a difficult decision. The original may play a key roll in honoring the colorful nature of the source language. On the other hand, as with this proverb, it may be truer to the intent of the original to use the English equivalent and continue the flow of the scene.

Comedy Equivalents

Few areas in translation require greater liberties than humor. A seemingly innocuous phrase may be said with endearing and hilarious inflection, or a common cliché may be subtly changed to great effect. The translator must attempt to understand the humor of the source dialogue and find inventive ways to share the same comic touch in the subtitles. It's hit or miss, like all comedy, but delightful to try. In Episode 10 of *My Wife is a Superwoman*, Ji-ae and her daughter Jung-won give her husband a new tie:

JUNG-WON

Mommy got you a new tie.

My Wife is a Superwoman (2009)

DAL-SU

Whoa. For me? Looks pricey.

JI-AE

Jung-won, tell him I didn't buy it. It was a gift.

JUNG-WON

It was a present.

DAL-SU

Yeah? Pretty spiffy, don't you think?

JI-AE

Tell him you put a monkey in a suit, it's still a monkey.

JUNG-WON

You're a monkey.

Ji-ae does not say anything about monkeys. "Tell him it's wasted on a petty herring," or "A nice tie is wasted on a little herring," is closer to the source dialogue, but "herring" doesn't carry the same connotation in English as it does in the original. To say, "Such a nice tie is wasted on such a petty person" completely loses the bantering tone. The subtitles use an English equivalent, "put a monkey in a suit." Jung-won's helpful interpretation is especially funny with this variation, going from the source dialogue, "it's a waste" to "you're a monkey." Just as the source did, the English equivalent uses an animal to make the point—he's not worth the tie he's wearing. In the same episode, a character asks Ji-ae what she would do if her husband had an affair:

> He'd better be sneaky. Cause the second I catch him...
> He'll die 'til he's dead!

"Die 'til he's dead" makes no sense, but has been a comedy staple since it was made famous in Disney's *Robin Hood* (1973). It perfectly captures the tone of the original, which might literally be translated as, "I'll kill him and kill him!"

Syntax. Subtitles should communicate a character's unique syntax and idiomatic variations. Sometimes this requires taking a few liberties that, ironically, are truer to the screenplay than a literal translation. The comic relief character in *Time Between Dog & Wolf* doesn't so much speak his lines as revel in them. There's no outright laughs, but plenty of chuckles at the way Ahwa says things just a little off from what's expected. He's greedy, loves to hang around tough guys and is a coward except when cheering a kickboxing match. He's young, but fancies himself a crusty old trainer, which is part of the joke.

It would be shamefully easy to toss in the usual American slang for someone Ahwa's age, but that would fail this dense, plodding, amoral yet loveable character. Surfer dude dialogue, for example, would come off as witless rather than witty.

The following excerpts compare a literal translation to subtitles that replicate as best possible Ahwa's posturing. These examples are from scenes in which he stands ringside and cheers the main hero, Kay, who's doing the real fighting. In later episodes, Ahwa adopts exaggerated organized crime lingo. Where the true criminals have terse, genuinely chilling dialogue, the comic character's speech is slightly off-key.

Literal	True-to-Character
Show him what you can do.	Give him a little taste..!
Beat him up, Kay!	Lay down a beatin', Kay!
I'm getting rich tonight!	Daddy's bringing home the bacon tonight!
Now you can beat him up..!	Time to hand out a beatin'..!
He's a weak opponent!	This guy hits like a girl!
Try your backspin kick.	See how he likes a little backspin kick.
That was great! Now rest a little. A little more. That was a good round but now... it's time to beat up this weak person.	That was great! Take a breather... that's it... That was good but now... time to lay him out.
You made me lose a lot of money. You were beating him up and then what? KO! Tell me what happened. Answer me! He was weak and deserved to be defeated. What happened to you?	You lost me a ton of cash. You were smacking him around and then bam! KO! What happened, I wanna know. Answer me! That sissy had a beatin' comin'. What's got into you?

Childlike & Childish

Childlike subtitles are full of wonder and discovery. They charm and enchant the viewer. Childish subtitles grate. Both have their place.

Adults. A character behaving childishly will have dialogue filled with "I" and "me". The subtitles should be clipped, laden with accusatory phrasing. In contrast, some adult characters adopt a childlike tone when speaking with the very young. Subtitles may use such terms as "yummy" and "does your tummy feel bad?" Observe how adults speak to their own children to capture the unique cadence of loving families.

The adult child. Many programs have quiet childlike moments. Adults rediscover something and express it in brief yet elegantly mature terms. Another type of adult child commonly appears in horror films as a heroic figure, as in Stephen King's *The Stand*. Tom Cullen is mentally disabled. He is a noble character inhibited by the challenges of his condition. Observe how King effortlessly captures Tom's childlike faith:

> The Lord is my shepherd. I shall not want for nothing. He makes me lie down in the green pastures. He greases up my head with oil. He gives me kung-fu in the face of my enemies. Amen.

The dialogue communicates much about the character without battering the reader. It does not view Tom as an oddity, but instead fills his words with meaning. This type of adult child is particularly difficult to translate. The source is often written in a deceptively simple style that should be replicated in the subtitles. Simplify but never pander. Let the words speak to the beauty of the character.

Children. The better films are populated with children whose dialogue has the fanciful rhythms of young people who speak in their own voices while at the same time trying to sound just a little more grown-up. In Episode 51 of *East of Eden*, the young boy Tae-ho interrupts one of his parents' frequent arguments. The adults say they are sorry. Tae-ho replies:

> Why're you both always sorry? How about more love, less sorries? Is it my fault? You can tell me though.

The subtitles should sound like a child without being whiny. The translation uses vernacular common to young children, such as making up a conjunction ("why're") or a word like "sorries." The boy is speaking to adults and tries to speak like them—in childlike fashion. "More this, less that" is an adult couplet the child has often heard, as is the addition of "though" at the end of a sentence. Viewers will recognize the childlike speech patterns: brief, simple and poignant.

Foreign Phrases

There are certain non-English phrases that work very well in English subtitles after they are introduced. Others must be translated.

Organizations. Many organization names translate perfectly well. National Tax Bureau, for example. However, some organizations sound much better in their original tongue and may be used in subtitles with little discomfort to the audience. Samurai has long since entered the English language, so it is not difficult for viewers to understand the Korean Hwarang, an elite fighting corps that plays a key role in *Queen Seondeok*. The dialogue makes much use of the term and it belongs in the subtitles.

One-offs. Some terms are explained so explicitly in the source dialogue, it's fitting to use them in their original form, as in Episode 1 of *Queen Seondeok*, when two women observe the Hwarang painting their faces:

SOHWA

They're so pretty. Prettier than me, even.

MAYA

You don't know a *nangjang* when you see it.

SOHWA

My Lady?

MAYA

When Hwarang paint their faces it's called a *nangjang*. You've never heard of it?

SOHWA

What does it mean?

MAYA

They are preparing to die. The Hwarang paint their faces on the eve of a battle or an important mission. So they'll be handsome, even in death.

The term is clearly defined. It adds historical verisimilitude to the subtitles just as it did for the original viewing audience. This is rare, however.

Using phrases from the source language can be a sloppy translation habit that stands in the way of viewers' enjoyment of a film. Terms may be unique to a given language, but emotions are universal. The subtitler must find English expressions that resonate with the same power.

Special words. Some words carry thematic weight. They deserve careful attention in subtitles, such as the final scene in French from Edmond Rostand's play, *Cyrano de Bergerac:*

> Quelque chose que sans un pli, sans une tache,
> J'emporte malgré vous, et c'est... Mon panache.

Carol Clark explains the difficulties of translating the hero's dying words:

> There is only one word in the play which is really untranslatable, and that is, unfortunately the final and most important word—*panache.* Its primary meaning is a plume. . . . But by the early twentieth century it had acquired in French the secondary meaning of dash or swagger. . . . Cyrano's dying words—'*mon panache*'—must refer to the actual plume on his hat, since he speaks of doffing it and sweeping the floor of heaven with it. But it also seems to refer metaphorically to some defining aspect of his character. . . . Finding an English equivalent for this totemic object, and at the same time a concluding rhyme, was, I am afraid, beyond me.

This is one of those rare cases when an English equivalent may not be required. In the film and play versions of *Cyrano de Bergerac,* the visual reference to the plume is absolutely clear. Using "panache" in subtitles gives proper weight to the actual meaning while adding a dash of, well, panache.

Borrowed words. The source dialogue may have a borrowed English word, but some terms don't travel well from one language to another. For example, Japanese colloquial expression refers to a condominium as a *manshon.* Condominium renovations are *manshon reformu.* Condominiums at hot spring resorts are *spaman* (spa plus *manshon*). Transcribing *manshon* as mansion doesn't work. If a character matter-of-factly states to his mother, "Here's my condo," a subtitle that reads "Here's my mansion" would be misconstrued as sardonic or self-effacing. In Korea, men's briefs and women's panties are grouped together under a single word for underpants, "panty." If a serious discussion about purchasing a pair of men's briefs is underway, a subtitle that reads, "He's old-fashioned—conservative panties would be best," is completely wrong. Do not transcribe unless the word has the same usage in both languages.

Other words travel back and forth between languages to take on lives of their own. Karaoke has entered English speech and needs no translation. Pronounced kalah-okay, the word stems from a Japanese linguistic mix-n-match: *kara,* meaning "empty" (as in *karate*—"empty hand") and *oke,* a shortened form of orchestra. Combined they translate as "empty orchestra" or simply "no band." Both the meaning and the word have made their way to America, where it is pronounced "carry-okee" in a cultural adoption not unlike the way orchestra became *oke* in Japan.

In Korea, the English word "Fighting!" has entered common speech as an equivalent of "Go get 'em!" In film the meaning is so unquestionably clear that it's jarring to see and hear a character say in English, "Fighting!" (often pronounced "hwaiting") only to have subtitles translate it as "Go for it" or any number of dull variations. This is a borrowed word that has a unique charm. It belongs in the subtitles exactly as spoken on screen.

So continues the quixotic and paradoxical globalization of language.

International language. American and British English are different, of course, but in general variations are negligible outside the areas of slang, jargon and idiomatic expressions. Linguist Charles L. Barber observed: "In grammar and syntax, the differences between British and American usage are not great . . . in all essentials, British and American syntax are identical." Some terms have entered into the world's common language. "Ninja," or "internet," for example. Certainly "jawohl" in films with Nazi villains. *Monsieur, mademoiselle, senora, senor, senorita, herr* and *fräulein* are known by most filmgoers. Agatha Christie gave *Death on the Nile* a remarkable verisimilitude in her dialogue for Hercule Poirot:

> Mademoiselle, I beseech you, do not do what you are doing. . . . Do not open your heart to evil. Because—if you do—evil will come. . . . It will enter in and make its home within you and after a while it will no longer be possible to drive it out.

Screenwriter Anthony Shaffer knew the value of a well-placed non-English word in his adaptation for John Guillermin's *Death on the Nile* (1978). He retains *mademoiselle* as delivered by Peter Ustinov:

> I must warn you, mademoiselle: do not allow evil into your heart, it will make a home there.

David Suchet's delivery of Kevin Elyot's dramatization is even shorter in Andy Wilson's *Poirot: Death on the Nile* (2004). The *mademoiselle* remains:

> Do not open your heart to evil, mademoiselle. If you do there will be no turning back.

David Suchet as Hercule Poirot

Some terms lend flavor from the original without being confusing. They belong in subtitles. Quentin Tarantino knew this when he wrote his own subtitles for *Inglourious Basterds*, including "oui" rather than the translation, "yes." The actor says "oui" and the subtitle reads "oui." Audiences know what "oui" means: it is evocative of the French setting and enhances enjoyment of the film. Translate every word of the screenplay—that's a subtitler's job. But alert the editor and producer of alternatives. Be mindful of the growing international language.

Translators choose words everyday. The best subtitles serve as a bridge between cultures while remaining as true as possible to the tone, style and words of the original. The subtitler must honor dialogue and context within the time and space available—and so at times must choose non-literal expressions to best communicate the intent of the film and its characters.

Chapter Four

Style

REPORTER

Are you a mod or a rocker?

RINGO

I'm a mocker.

—*A Hard Day's Night* (1964)

Films are pop culture. There is great art in any medium, but ultimately a subtitle translator is part of the entertainment business. Gossip columnist Louella Parsons' observation in 1935 holds true today: "Art is simply fine in Hollywood—if it pays dividends." But this does not excuse shoddy work. Quite the opposite, as Luciano Pavarotti pointed out:

> Some say the word 'pop' is a derogatory word to say 'not important'—I do not accept that. If the word 'classic' is the word to say 'boring', I do not accept. There is good and bad music.

Pavarotti illustrated his point in a genre-crossing career of worldwide appeal. Leo Tolstoy also noted that popularity does not preclude greatness:

> I rather like it. This swift change of scene, this blending of emotion and experience—it is much better than the heavy, long-drawn-out kind of writing to which we are accustomed. It is closer to life. In life, too, changes and transitions flash by before our eyes, and emotions of the soul are like a hurricane. The cinema has divined the mystery of motion. And that is greatness.

When Correct Grammar is Wrong-*ish*

Subtitles model the grammar of the original dialogue—right, wrong or indifferent. This is not to suggest that proper grammar does not have its place.

Proper Usage

A subtitler must know proper English usage before daring to alter it, just as a jazz musician launches into thematic variations from a solid foundation of technical expertise. What's true for language and music is equally true with film grammar. From the grandmaster of muscular movies, John Huston:

> I have been speaking of style, but before there can be style, there must be grammar. There is, in fact, a grammar to picture-making. The laws are as inexorable as they are in language. . . . They must, of course, be disavowed and disobeyed from time to time, but one must be aware of their existence.

Huston observed that knowledge of film techniques comes before variations in style. This is equally true with language. Indeed, the translator's burden is doubled—a subtitler must be proficient in the source and target languages. Only after learning the rules of usage in both may a translator capably communicate grammatical variations in subtitles.

Never Correct the Original

In *I Really, Really Like You*, the First Lady and her son, Dr. Jang, have a studied, correct style of speech that is always proper in the original script. The subtitles display this by decreasing the number of conjunctions, eliminating slang, and at times using terms that might seem a bit stuffy with anyone other than these characters. In Episode 20 the middle-aged First Lady refers to Bong-sun's boyfriend as "your young man." Similarly, in Episode 26, Dr. Jang uses the informed lingo of a connoisseur:

> Wine is difficult to explain, complex and delicate. It was vibrant on my tongue, slightly bitter on the finish.

An educated tone can also come off as arrogant. In Episode 23, an assistant accuses the head chef of having a "cavalier manner", which captures the original's cumbersome phrase and the dialogue's accusatory tone. Grammatical propriety can be subtle. In Episode 19, the president and head chef jokingly bicker about which of them cared for the young heroine as a baby. "Do you know that I'm the one that reared you?" asks the chef. "The President saved and raised me," she answers.

I Really, Really Like You (2006)

This dialogue distinction illustrates that a mountain girl might use the colloquial "raise" while the president and chef, educated men, would use the grammatically correct "rear". Meaning is as much a question of usage as definition. Linguistic scholar Deborah Cameron:

> . . . people do not learn most words from dictionaries but infer their meanings from hearing them used in particular contexts: we may all differ slightly in our beliefs about what words 'really mean' . . . because the meaning of words is ultimately a matter of the way the community uses them in talk. Unless they are compulsive users of dictionaries, this will be determined by contextual inference, and meaning will be inherently unstable.

In *East of Eden*, a comic character frequently mutters what everyone else is thinking but dares not say. Her dialogue is endearingly straight-forward but laced with the rustic speech patterns of her country background, as in Episode 45, when she shakes her head at the plot's mismatched identities:

> Ugh. I can't keep up with who's related to who anymore.

Of course, "who's related to whom" is proper usage, but few people speak that way—particularly not comic relief. Improper grammar is exactly right in capturing the character's bantering charm. Never correct the original.

Trite and True. Many common expressions are poor grammar, but because they persist, audiences are used to them. When a trite phrase occurs in the original, a similar English cliché may suit. The viewer's eyes will immediately register the well-worn expression and the flow of the scene will move forward. One example is the use of rhetoric in courtroom dramas, from *Perry Mason* to *Law & Order*. It often goes like this:

> Lawyer: Isn't it true you were at the corner of Cliché and Trite?
> Suspect: No, I wasn't.

This is atrocious grammar. The correct answer is either, "Yes, it is not true," or "No, it is true." However, "isn't it true" is so common in US courtroom dramas that viewers will unquestionably recognize it as TV legal talk. Translating this as "Were you at the corner of Cliche and Trite?" is accurate, clear and proper, but lacks the legalese flavor audiences enjoy.

Transcribing English. Occasionally actors speak in the subtitle's target language—for this book, English. They may not be fluent. Their pronunciation may be difficult to follow. Transcribe the English exactly as spoken. If there are grammatical errors, include them. Word-for-word. It is not a subtitler's place to correct grammar, in translation or transcription.

The Joy of Language

"All modern American literature comes from one book by Mark Twain called *Huckleberry Finn*," wrote Ernest Hemingway in *Green Hills of Africa*. ". . . it's the best book we've had. All American writing comes from that." Readers may argue Hemingway's point but there is no doubt *The Adventures of Huckleberry Finn* has significantly influenced American colloquial speech. Twain's dialogue is precise. It is pure. Grammatical improprieties are legion, but never spurious or trivial. Twain loved language, toyed with it, reveled in it. There is no excess. He chose his words carefully. In doing so, he gave readers as perfect an image of a sunrise as the English language can provide:

> Not a sound anywheres—perfectly still—just like the whole world was asleep, only sometimes the bullfrogs a-cluttering, maybe. The first thing to see, looking away over the water, was a kind of dull line—that was the woods on t'other side; you couldn't make nothing else out; then a pale place in the sky; then more paleness spreading around; then the river softened up away off, and warn't black any more, but gray; you could see little dark spots drifting along ever so far away—trading scows, and such things; and long black streaks—rafts; sometimes you could hear a sweep screaking; or jumbled up voices, it was so still, and sounds come so far; and by and by you could see a streak on the water which you know by the look of the streak that there's a snag there in a swift current which breaks on it and makes that streak look that way; and you see the mist curl up off of the water, and the east reddens up, and the river, and you make out a log-cabin in the edge of the woods, away on the bank on t'other side of the river, being a woodyard, likely, and piled by them cheats so you can throw a dog through it anywheres; then the nice breeze springs up, and comes fanning you from over there, so cool and fresh and sweet to smell on account of the woods and the flowers; but sometimes not that way, because they've left dead fish laying around, gars and such, and they do get pretty rank; and next you've got the full day, and everything smiling in the sun, and the song-birds just going it!

Any subtitler—any writer—would be proud to pen such prose. Twain is the best example of how improper grammar can be the right choice for natural character voice. Again from John Huston: "Whatever action takes place on that screen must not violate our sense of the appropriate." A subtitler must always search for phrasing appropriate to the script and genre. Good grammar or not.

The Adventures of Huckleberry Finn (1960)

Notes on Style

Every translator should own a copy of *The Elements of Style* by William Strunk, Jr. and E. B. White and *The Elements of Grammar* by Margaret Shertzer. The following notes are specific to the requirements of subtitling, but no rule is absolute, as noted by poet, playwright and translator Edwin Honig:

> Whatever translators think, their work cannot proceed simply from a single theory about how to do it. The complex and irrational serving of exigency while calibrating word-by-word minutiae makes them uncomfortable with all theories. Nor do mottoes help muffle the small crushing voice they hear whispering, 'What you're doing is ridiculous because it's absolutely impossible.' . . . What is one's relation to a job—a job one wants to do well? One must first believe it can be done. But how is the belief sustained through all the self-abnegations of translation and mistranslation is a psychological mystery only translators themselves can reveal—and then only partially.

Style

Be aware of tone. Subtle differences can have a dramatic impact on how viewers perceive a scene. A subtitler must know the original film's characters and context before making translation choices. Be concise.

Match style to character. Subtitles should match the style of delivery. Choose vigorous phrasing by default—it's usually shorter and fits the scene adequately. However, a character's personality may demands weaker words. Study the script to know which translation serves the viewers:

> He's someone I could be happy with; *or*
> He's someone with whom I could be happy.

In both cases, the "he" in question is the focus of the dialogue. Changing it to "I could be happy with him" is completely wrong. Listen to the actor's reading of the part; study the character and the script to decide which style suits a scene. Each says something different about the speaker:

> I have been happy in the past; *or*
> I used to be happy; *or*
> I was happy once.

The first is informative; the second whining; the third wistful. Note subtle differences and match them to the script and delivery of the original.

Negatives. Language is riddled with them, liberally sprinkled in a way that makes perfect sense in spoken dialogue but can be cumbersome in written form. Use negatives sparingly, according to the source language, but remember that often an equivalent is equally clear. If the speaker seems unsure or accusatory, use the negative:

Aren't you happy?

If the question is merely interrogative, prefer the positive:

Are you happy?

Break sentences in two. Sometimes a long-winded character's lines must be connected with dots; other times a clean break is required:

I wanted to tell you earlier...
that I'm pregnant.

The dots indicate a continuation from one screen to the next. The character paused mid-sentence. In this presentation, the important revelation is weakened. Better to break the sentence in two for full impact, just as it was in the original:

I wanted to tell you earlier...
I'm pregnant.

Here the dots indicate trailing off, a lingering pause. "I wanted to tell you earlier that..." is even worse. Remove the unnecessary word and the scene retains its power.

Fragments. Dialogue is riddled with speech fragments: thoughts half-said, pauses, explanations. From Strunk and White: "Generally speaking, the place for broken sentences is in dialogue, when a character happens to speak in a clipped or fragmentary way."

Spelling. Dialogue often uses colloquial speech. For example, Major Eaton in *Raiders of the Lost Ark* asks, "Alright, now, what do you mean the Ten Commandments, you talking about THE Ten Commandments?" Margaret Shertzer states that "alright" does not exist in that spelling. "All right [is] the correct form," she writes. However, "alright" saves two character spaces in subtitles and is exactly right for Eaton. Observe colloquial usage.

Match the tense. Past, present, future: be sure the subtitles match the tense of the dialogue. "He says he loves you" has a distinctly different tone from "He said he loves you." The first is intimate, immediate. The second a simple repetition. Note the subtleties of the script to give proper tense.

Clichés and stereotypes. If the original uses a source language cliché, an English equivalent may be necessary. Clichés have a bad name. They are trite, true, but they are invaluable as background filler in many scenes. The cranky old man. The drunk. The bitter waitress. The pushy salesperson. These stereotypes are immediately recognizable to viewers. If they are walk-on parts, there simply to move the plot forward or be background for the protagonists, use subtitles that match their trite dialogue. Do not call attention to them with unexpected phrasing. If the original script fills their mouths with the usual banalities, the subtitles should do the same.

Capitalization of titles. Generally, capitalize proper nouns—that is, nouns that refer to a specific place, object, idea or person. Capitalization must be uniform. If all other rulers are "kings" but the current head of state is always called, "the King," then be sure this rule applies to the subtitles throughout the program. If a son calls his father "Dad" in direct address, don't switch to lower-case later. Also, choose "Dad" or "Father" and stick to it. Rules of proper usage apply, but in subtitles there may be a few variations. An odd spelling may be used to indicate the dialogue's nuanced reference to a specific person, a sort of tonal capitalization. Once introduced, this usage may be used to represent that particular character. Equally, capitalization can be used to show formality or emphasis. When two crooks discuss a king, any king, lower-case is fine. When two ministers whisper, "The King won't be happy," upper-case indicates this formal phrasing and alerts viewers that the person in question is the same "King" (upper-case) they've been watching so far. The inflection gives the title proper noun status. In a modern example, company presidents don't get the same consideration as heads-of-state. Preceding a name, use upper-case:

> President Jones and President Smith will be there.

Otherwise, reserve upper-case for the head of state:

> All the company presidents are ordered to attend the meeting with the President.

Unique capitalization should be used with great economy, but it can be a useful way to keep titles straight and indicate tone and intent. They give viewers the cues they need to follow who's talking about whom. The same rule applies to phrases identifying key religious ideas. "The mandate of Heaven" or "the temple of Karnak" is proper. However, if the characters use the term in hushed tones, "Temple of Karnak" communicates the character's reverential awe. After introducing Karnak's importance in the subtitles, "the Temple" may be used to indicate the edifice. If the term's religious significance plays a key role, "Mandate of Heaven" brings attention to that fact. It gives weight equal to the verbal emphasis in the dialogue.

Exclamation points! Use only when yelling! They are distracting! A little goes a long way. Do not emphasize simple statements or commands with an exclamation point. Let the character's tone speak for itself.

Onomatopoeia. Characters moan and sigh. Usually it's obvious in context and no subtitle is needed. However, viewers do not know the source language and so may not be aware that a certain sound is a groan of exasperation. In those cases, choose brief English equivalents, such as "ugh" or "whew" to alert the audience that the sound is nothing more.

Lyrics, Poetry, Voice-overs and Quotations

Lyrics. A song should be translated when the lyric applies to a specific scene or the overall theme of the film. If it merely sets the mood, subtitling is unnecessary. Separate lyrics from spoken dialogue with italics or quotation marks.

Poetry. If reciting a poem written by another person, use quotation marks. If a poem is the character's own, no indicator is needed.

Voice-overs. If the voice-over is a narration throughout the program, do not italicize. If it is an internal monologue within a conversation between characters, italicize to indicate which is spoken and which is thought. If it is an internal monologue while a character is alone, italics are not necessary.

Flashbacks. Flashbacks may be indicated by single quotation marks or italics. If the flashback is from a scene that aired earlier in a series, the phrasing must match the previous subtitles exactly.

Quotation marks. Quotation marks can be powerful when used with economy.

> *Mimicry.* Often dialogue is spoken with a snide mimicry, a kind of verbal quotation mark: "Suddenly you're all 'gotta ask me first'?"
> *Quoting others.* "Remember when the doctor said, 'You've got two months'?" is much more immediate than "Do you remember when the doctor said you have two months?" Study the source dialogue, particularly the actor's delivery, to see if a direct quote suits the tone.

Dots

Dots are part and parcel of the subtitling craft. Audiences are accustomed to them and understand their purpose. Used with precision, dots are an invaluable tool. Ellipsis is a term for three or more dots separated by one space each to indicate missing text: ". . ." Prefer period dots without spaces: "..."

Continuing from one screen to the next. Perhaps the most common use of dots—and the least standardized. Some distributors prefer three dots at the end of a line, but not the beginning of the next:

> Tell me why you're so anxious...
> why won't you give in?

Other distributors use dots to indicate the second line is a continuation of the first:

> Tell me why you're so anxious...
> ...why won't you give in?

Or to indicate the line is in the middle of a longer sentence:

> Tell me...
> ...why you're so anxious...
> ...why won't you give in?

This is also used when two characters are speaking and one finishes the sentence of the other:

> So you're nervous because...
> ...my folks are coming, yes.

Both are acceptable, but the latter is impractical for long speeches.

Long speeches. When screen room is at a premium dots take up three valuable character spaces. With long speeches, break the line at the breath points, according to the actor's natural pacing. Use dots at the end of the line to indicate continuation, beginning the next screen with a lower-case letter. Often long speeches use two lines on a single screen. Dots alert viewers that the second line is connected to the first:

> Lower-case letters in the subsequent line...
> indicate a continuation from the first.

Depending on the time available, two lines may be used per screen. Three lines are distracting.

Pauses. Often a character will pause when confused, unable to continue, or prior to a major plot revelation. Unlike speeches, these pauses are concerned with timing more than space. Pace subtitles to the speech patterns of the actors:

> I'm not so sure... well...
> It's just when you say that I think...
> you're right.

The first line uses dots to trail off. The last two lines are connected by dots at the end of the second and a lower case at the beginning of the third.

Cut-offs and trail-offs. Sometimes characters are surprised or dread finishing a sentence. They cut off their own dialogue. Use two dots followed by appropriate punctuation to indicate this:

> You don't mean..?
> I won't allow..! Wait, say that again?

Comic characters mumble, dramatic characters get confused, words trail off into nothing or remain half-spoken:

> Wha..? Who could've..? I'm not sure...

The line immediately following should begin with an upper-case letter. Combined with the pace of the spoken dialogue and the context of the scene, the intent will be clear.

Interjections. Characters talk over each other. They interrupt. They continue the other's sentences. Use dots when the first speaker is unsure or muttering:

> - I'm just sayin' is all...
> - How 'bout you don't next time?

For strident interruptions use a long dash:

> - But mommy said—
> - Dinner ready yet?

The short dash indicates that both lines of dialogue will appear on the same screen, on top of each other. This standard format is easy to follow with the eye. It gives the subtitles and the audience much-needed time.

A Few General Specifications

There are no absolute rules in spotting. They vary between distributors. However, most follow something close to this standard:

> No more than 1 character per 2 frames
> Each subtitle displayed about 1.5 seconds on average
> Rows must fit within 80% of the width of the picture
> NTSC video - No more than 40-45 characters per line
> PAL video - No more than 34 characters per line
> No more than 2 lines per screen
> Arial is the standard font for most English subtitles
> Justify center

Names

A subtitler has a number of choices regarding character names:

Choosing a name. Some names are too long. Miyamoto Musashi, for example, is a solid name in Japanese but takes up valuable space in subtitles. Shortening it to Musashi is the obvious solution. It has the added benefit of reading well in English. A solid heroic name. Consider the villain's name in *Raiders of the Lost Ark* (1981): René Emile Belloq. When Indiana Jones spits out "Belloq" it's like he's coughing up something nasty.

Non-family family names. Some languages resist the use of a person's name in preference to a title or a term that defines the relationship between the speakers. "Older brother," for example, can be used in some cultures to refer to one's blood brother, an older male friend or even a boyfriend. In these situations, using "bro" in subtitles never works. It's dated, forced, and comes off as glib and affected. Better to avoid the reference altogether and use the character's proper name. When the appellation is an accurate description of the family relationship, however, it may be used in scenes of great emotional impact, but sparingly.

Shortening the name. Short names are not always available, but the whole name is rarely possible in subtitles, even when characters repeat it relentlessly. Some languages lean more easily to repetition than English. Languages that seldom use personal pronouns, preferring titles and names, fall in this category:

> Professor Shibata, why are you doing that? What kind of
> man are you, Professor? Isn't it a little late to be eating ice
> cream, Professor Shibata?

Shortening names and titles decreases the space required for subtitles:

> Professor, what are you up to? What kind of man are you?
> Isn't it a little late for ice cream?

This dialogue illustrates the snobbery of the speaker, stressing status in contrast to snacking on ice scream. The subtitles must include "professor" at least once to communicate this point but its repetition serves no thematic purpose. It may be discarded.

You. Translator Robin Buss explained: "Every European language except English (in which 'thee' and 'thou' have long been archaic except in some dialects) has kept the second person singular for use with intimates, close friends and relatives." Many languages have varying levels of formality attached to the word *you*, employing different terms for essentially the same meaning. This is illustrated in the Buss translation of Alexandre Dumas' *The Count of Monte Cristo*:

The Count of Monte Cristo (1908)

MONTE CRISTO

You know, Haydée...

HAYDÉE

Why do you not say *tu* to me, as usual? Have I done something wrong? In that case, I must be punished, but don't say *vous* to me.

Compare this to the anonymous translation published in 1846, which sidesteps the forms of address completely:

MONTE CRISTO

Haydée, you well know.

HAYDÉE

Why do you address me so coldly—so distantly? Have I by any means displeased you? Oh, if so, punish me as you will; but do not—do not speak to me in tones and manner so formal and constrained!

Buss asserted the 1846 translation "makes very little sense here, because Monte Cristo has said only three words (four in the translation) since entering the room, which is frankly not enough to provide grounds for her accusation. The point is that one of the three words is the formal, second person plural, *vous*." Buss had a point. Observe the telltale *tu* and *vous* in the original French:

MONTE CRISTO

Haydée, dit-il, vous savez...

HAYDEE

Pourquoi ne me dis-tu pas *tu* comme d'habitude ? ai-je donc commis quelque faute ? En ce cas il faut me punir, mais non pas me dire *vous*.

However, subtitles do not enjoy the luxury of space and time that is afforded literature. Explanatory notes do not belong on-screen. In *The Last Cavalier*, translator Lauren Yoder smoothly inserted a helpful explanation in the text itself:

'Can you tell me?' Spurred by curiosity, Mademoiselle was using the informal *tu* form with her friend Claire, though normally in conversation they used formal address.

This question of formal and intimate terms comes up frequently in subtitle translation. A character is miffed that his lover uses the standard form of *you* or, conversely, another is insulted when the intimate form is used inappropriately. Translating either simply as "you" would make any extreme reaction to the term jarring and out of place. Observe the context of the scene. If the man's lover uses the formal *you*, subtitles may represent this with stiffer phrasing and decreased conjunctions to indicate a stylistic change that is echoed in the actress' tone and delivery. If sudden intimacy is indicated, increasing conjunctions and using shorter, less structured expressions will replicate the impact of an informal *you*.

Nicknames. Nicknames often endear the speaker to the recipient and the audience. Or alienate an irritating character who uses derogatory euphemisms. Most nicknames are short, often humorous, but they rarely translate well. In the comedy series *Boys Over Flowers* (2009), the boys who are "prettier than flowers" all fall for a girl they nickname Dry Cleaning, referring to her parent's dry cleaning shop. The nickname is used throughout the program, first in juxtaposition to the relative social status of the characters and ultimately as a term of endearment. In subtitles, "Dry Cleaning" is stiff. "Laundry" isn't funny, either. "Laundromat," however, has the right comic twist. The family doesn't run a Laundromat, which makes the extravagantly wealthy boys' misnomer especially apt. It captures the baiting tone of the original. Dialogue often includes an explanation for a nickname, but even without it viewers sense the warmth, as when Jean Gabin calls René Dary "Porcupine Head" in the subtitles for Criterion's release of Jacques Becker's *Touchez pas au grisbi* (1954). Other nicknames serve translation well. If everyone refers to a pest as Smelly in the original, "Stinky" is a succinct and funny equivalent.

Use the same name. Introduce a character with the whole name, if used, but after that choose a shorter version and stick with it. If the program focuses on mistaken or false identities, follow the script closely. Trust the screenplay to explain everything—and trust the viewers to understand it.

Use uniform spelling. There is much discussion among translators about using a Romanization system or writing the name the way it sounds. Romanization methodology is usually prepared by scholars interested in developing a complete system to approximate sounds and combinations. Romanization is invaluable, but there is a learning curve involved. Any learning done by film viewers must be in the subtitles. The least painful route is using a sound-alike system—writing the names so that when read they sound like the original. This allows the audience to say a name and listen for it in the dialogue. Both approaches have their adherents and both serve important roles in translation. Whichever is used, be sure that the spelling and methodology is uniform.

Titles. Some supporting characters are better known by their titles. If Professor Shibata is only on-screen now and then to support the main action as a teacher or a wise advisor, use his full name once, then "Professor" after. Titles also say much about the speakers using them. In the historical epic *Queen Seondeok*, the dialogue is filled with references to Field Marshal Munno. Everyone talks about him. The king and nobles call him Munno. Members of the military corps, the Hwarang, refer to him as, "The Field Marshal." This is easily represented in subtitles. The question of royalty is a little trickier. All of the characters use the same form of address for the king, but their relationships are quite different and the language is filled with inflections and nuances that demonstrate that fact. The nobles serve the king but are jockeying for power. The Hwarang have sworn personal fealty to the royal house. They answer their supervising officers as "sir," but to illustrate the unique relationship with the royal family, the Hwarang subtitles use "My Lord" or "My Lady" when addressing the king or queen. Nobles address the king as "Sire." This alerts the viewers that the inflections and relationships are slightly different.

Place Names, Signs & Text

Written information. Anytime the camera lingers on written information that is not read aloud by the characters, the relevant points must be translated. Distributors use a variety of formats. The most common:

MAIN STREET   [The Old Man and the Sea]
<Man Wins Lottery>   (Ella's House of Jazz)

Title cards, intertitles and subtitles in the source language. Any words that flash on the screen must be translated. Often this is informative:

<The Metropolitan Police Service. London.>

Some historical dramas flash a note, as in Episode 19 of *Queen Seondeok*:

Deokman's a sly one. She may 'Feint east and strike west'.
<Strategy 6 of *The 36 Stratagems*>

This bracketed note was part of the original airing and must be translated. Such bracketed explainers should not be inserted by the subtitler unless they exist in the source program, with the exception of establishing shots.

Dashes. In written information, use a dash rather than the word "to":

<Luke 2: 8-10>

In dialogue, it must be spelled out:

He read the second chapter of Luke, verses eight to ten.

The Great Queen Seondeok (2009)

Establishing Shots. This basic of film grammar is designed to alert viewers of the location in which the subsequent scene will unfold. Generic office buildings, homes, warehouses and schools require no translation. If the location name is essential to the plot or unique in itself, such as the White House, insert the relevant information the first time the establishing shot is used. For television programs, identify specific locations the first time they appear in each episode.

Symbols & Numerals

Trust viewers to understand common symbols that, in fairness, they use everyday anyway. Spell out dates and numbers.

Money and amounts. Whether using the source currency or US dollars, a monetary symbol decreases space required for the subtitle. "$" is inert. Viewers see its intent and move on. Anything $10,000 or higher may be abbreviated to $10K, $100K, etc. Amounts higher than 1,000,000 usually receive a lot of attention, so they are best written exactly ($3,750,000) or as spoken: "One million dollars, wow."

Distances. Identify the clearest, briefest way to communicate well-known abbreviated symbols. Use them sparingly and according to uniform rules. 100 miles is fine. 100 kilometers is cumbersome. Shorten to 100km.

Quantities. 200lbs is fine, as is 30oz. 200 pounds or 30 ounces, not so much.

1st, 2nd, 3rd, etc. These may be used when space is tight, but judiciously. "He took 1st place," is perfectly clear. Use "first" when beginning or ending a sentence: "First, we need money," and "He came in first." As a general rule, "1st" is best used to indicate placement. Otherwise, spell it out.

Numerals. Never begin or end a sentence with a numeral unless counting:

Time for push-ups. 1... 2... 3... 4...

Avoiding using numerals for numbers *less than ten*:

- How many fingers am I holding up?
- Two.

Use numerals for *amounts over ten* and *street addresses*:

Our report indicates 117 items were stolen from 219 Park Street.

However, street names should be spelled out:

The accident was at First and Broadway.

Acronyms and Abbreviations

Abbreviations. An abbreviation does not spell a new word. When abbreviations arise in dialogue, such as with organizations, state the full name once and afterward use the abbreviation.

Acronyms. An acronym is an abbreviation that spells something. If it is used in the original dialogue, the subtitler may find an English equivalent to communicate the pun. For example, in Episode 11 of *My Wife is a Superwoman* Choi Yang-nak confronts a new member of the local sauna:

YANG

You got the boot, yeah?

JUN-HYUK

Me? Nuh-uh.

YANG

It's obvious, why deny it?

JUN-HYUK

I'm not denying nothin'. I'm here by choice.

YANG

Everyone says that at first. 'Here by choice.' I'm here by choice, too, come to that. 'Course she salted the earth and changed the locks. How's that not being kicked out?

JUN-HYUK

That's not me. I'm here to teach my wife a lesson.

YANG

Still making excuses. Haven't hit rock bottom yet. You can come to our WiMP meeting later. 'Women and the Men they Punish.'

JUN-HYUK

Nobody kicked me out.

YANG

$5 to join.

The dialogue is comic. The men in the sauna meeting sit around and complain about their wives. A literal translation of the group's acronym name lacks flair: "It's called K-O-M. Kicked-Out-Men." In English, KOM is an abbreviation. "WiMP" replicates the style and intent of the original.

My Wife is a Superwoman (2009)

What to Leave Out

A subtitler must translate every word of the spoken dialogue. However, not every word need end up on the screen.

Crowd scenes. Many crowd scenes are murmuring and chatter. Others are filled with such stereotypical invective that to put them in subtitles seems pointless. In the pilot episode of *The No. 1 Ladies' Detective Agency* (2008), a village open-air court begins with one line in subtitle:

> This man has stolen my cow.

The next thirty seconds—a full thirty—are filled with screaming plaintiffs, calming judges and observer comments, barely audible under the soundtrack. None of this is in the subtitles. More important to the plot, a young girl watching the proceedings has an idea. As the men argue, the girl runs down the road and returns with a calf. The calf nuzzles the cow.

> That's my calf! The calf knows its mother! That's proof!

Nothing more is needed. The arguing would detract from the point of the scene and fill the screen with irrelevancies.

Mobs. This rule also applies to most press mob scenes. An unlucky protagonist is surrounded by nameless reporters whose only role in the plot is to confront the hero with uncomfortable questions. None of the journalists will appear again. The scene may last as long as a minute while the hero plods through the mass of microphones and cameras. In this situation, less is definitely more. A few translated phrases serve the purpose, usually something like "How do you respond to the allegations?" or "Is it true you were involved?" or "Give us a comment!" A little insertion of the reporters' questions goes a long way. To include all the inquiries would fill the screen with subtitles that miss the point. Most scenes of this nature are intended to be background noise as the camera focuses on the protagonist.

Muffled conversation. Frequently conversations are muffled on purpose. The director intentionally leaves bits of dialogue inaudible. Subtitling them does the film and the viewers a disservice, as explained by Claire Denis:

> When we were shooting *Friday Night*, there is a scene where Valérie is in her car looking inside the café, watching the man drinking and speaking to the girl who is playing pinball. She is outside and wants to be inside. . .

The screenplay for *Friday Night* (2002) was written by Emmanuèle Bernheim and Denis, based on Bernheim's novel. The dialogue inside the café was barely audible in the film. However, the subtitler translated it anyway. Denis continued:

I asked the guy who did the subtitles if he could perhaps print them with one letter missing, or one word missing— as artists, you know. . . . And he said that that doesn't exist in subtitles. Either we have subtitles or we don't have subtitles.

Of course, Denis was right and the subtitler was wrong. A method of showing muffled dialogue belongs in the scene. For comic characters, "mmph-you don't-mph-do you?" could be used. For a dramatic scene, dots between scattered words may be effective. Viewers can hear that the dialogue is muffled. Subtitling every word is distracting.

Background chatter. Two characters are holding a conversation in a busy market. They ignore the noise around them in the urgency of their own troubles. The protagonists' dialogue belongs in subtitles. But translating the background chatter—"I'll have two of those," or "Thank you, how about another..?"—is senseless. It fills the screen with subtitles that detract from the focus of the scene. If background noise is relevant, it must be included. If chatter, leave it out. Subtitles must honor the director's choices.

Every word *must* be translated. However, the translator may suggest which lines might be left out. Ultimately, it is up to the distributor, but a subtitler's comments on which lines deserve prominence can be very helpful.

Edit

Subtitles may harm a movie. Few can ruin it. "I discovered early in my movie work that a movie is never any better than the stupidest man connected with it," wrote prolific Hollywood screenwriter Ben Hecht. The list of potential interlopers in the writer's original vision increases with international distribution. It includes the subtitler and an editor, as well as theater and home-release distributors. Even on the worst days—all translators have them—it's unlikely that weak subtitles will destroy a fine film. Audiences may sense there is something amiss, that there is much they are not getting, but the power of the film will still resonate. Hecht's comments on interfering producers apply to anyone involved in a film, including its subtitler:

Months later, watching 'my' movie in a theater, I realized that not much damage actually had been done. A movie is basically so trite and glib that the addition of a half dozen miserable inanities does not cripple it. It blares along barking out its inevitable clichés, and only its writer can know that it is a shade worse than it had to be.

Editors are frequently and unjustly maligned for the same reason that Hecht derided producers. Every subtitler works with an editor and spotter (except those souls forced to do all of the above). Jenna Johnson, senior editor at Houghton Mifflin Harcourt, discussed what she called "the cultural ambassadorship of an editor and translator," adding:

> Translators must act as representatives of the author's intentions, language, and style, but they must also be sensitive to the needs of readers in the target language. Editors here act as both the first reader and the first critic, working with translators to balance readability and integrity, fluidity of the new text and fidelity to the original.

Despite an often acrimonious relationship, a combination of separate skills can be advantageous to the end product. Kurosawa Akira's observations on writing are relevant to subtitlers and everyone else participating in the gestalt process of getting a film to the audience:

> In writing alone there is a danger that your interpretation of another human being will suffer from one-sidedness. If you write with two other people about that human being, you get at least three different viewpoints on him, and you can discuss the points on which you disagree.

Cursing

> I'm sorry if I offend you. But I don't swear just for the hell of it. You see, I figure language is a poor enough means of communication as it is. So we ought to use all the words we've got. Besides, there are damned few words that everybody understands.

> —*Inherit the Wind (1960)*

Cursing can stop a scene dead. If that is not the case in the original, there's no reason to include unnecessarily crude terms in the subtitles. Excrement, parentage and human copulation are all frequent sources of colorful euphemisms in many cultures. The translator's challenge is finding the correct balance that accurately communicates the tone, nuance and meaning of the source. This is not to say there is no place for curse words. They exist in the many films. Censoring dialogue in subtitles is unacceptable. However, absolute mastery of the target language is essential in choosing the right word that equates to the original's meaning and usage. From Wallace Stegner:

Words are not obscene: Naming things is a legitimate verbal act. And 'frank' does not mean 'vulgar,' any more than 'improper' means 'dirty.' What vulgar does mean is 'common'; what improper means is 'unsuitable'. Under the right circumstances, any word is proper. But when any sort of word, especially a word hitherto taboo and therefore noticeable, is scattered across a page like chocolate chips through a Toll House cookie, a real impropriety occurs. The sin is not the use of an 'obscene' word; it is the use of a loaded word in the wrong place or in the wrong quantity. It is the sin of false emphasis, which is not a moral but a literary lapse, related to sentimentality.

Consider these variations for identifying excrement: dooky, poop, poopy, stinky, crap, turd, dung, feces and of course shit. A character may be cursing or referring to the act itself. In either case an entirely different word must be used. Comic characters often speak sideways: "Drop a load" or "take a major" are clear without being too terribly crude, within a given context. Stephen King is one of the great cursing innovators of American English, as in *'salem's Lot*, when the constable mutters, "Floyd can crap in his hat and wear it backward for all of me." It's funny, inoffensive, and says much about the character. When dealing with curse words, it is essential to take stock of the scene:

- Is the curse word crude, humorous or descriptive?
- Is the character likely to use a crude word?
- In the context, is it necessary to use a crude term at all?

Parentage is another common source of crude language. In the proper context, bastard may be descriptive, entertaining or insulting. There's no denying that some expressions are ideally suited to their scenes. Few terms for a conniving traitor are better than "rat bastard"—it makes the point with great economy. Nor would many people change John Steinbeck's advice to John Kenneth Galbraith when the economist got a bad review: "I've always said that unless the bastards have the courage to give you unqualified praise, ignore them." In another context this term might be far too strong for the original dialogue.

Racial and Gender Slurs

Slurs are usually spoken by unsympathetic characters. A group of soldiers belittles a captive of a different race. Drunken men at a bar say ugly things about women. A group of women does the same about men. And on and on. Sometimes these slurs serve a purpose in establishing character and tone, or as foreshadowing of an epiphany or a comeuppance. Racial and gender slurs must be subtitled. Before translating, ask important questions:

1. Are the slurs gratuitous or do they serve the plot?
2. Do the slurs have equivalents that honor the intent without relying on crass phrases?
3. If the slurs must be used, are the English equivalents *exactly* right?

The last question is important. Finding equivalents is an inexact craft. If a slur is essential to the film, the English equivalent must have the same impact as the original dialogue. Not less. And certainly not more.

Variations

A subtitler should trust the viewers' mastery of their own native tongue. This is particularly true for comedies. For example, "son of a bitch" is always insulting, but is also an exclamation of frustration. Comic characters often mutter barely audible expletives. Audiences have seen this hundreds of times, so a simple "Sonuva..!" or "Piece of..!" communicates the original's intent and the nature of the aside without resorting to crudity. Joss Whedon explained his approach to cursing variants when asked about the word 'humped':

> I've always had it easy with language, because I'll always throw in a word that's not *quite* the word we're not supposed to use, but clearly means it. . . . I mean, I kept saying 'rutting' all the time and 'bunged', which if you really break it down, is even more impressive. In the early days of *Buffy*, I used British terms. And on *Firefly*, I used British, but usually Elizabethan terms, or terms that were made up to be ever so slightly different, but never any that would actually raise alarms, because nobody actually really seemed to know what they *meant*.

A translator must be aware of the target audience for a given entertainment. Television programs in America and their distributors have a single impossible goal: please everyone and offend no one. Of course, there are films and TV shows that go the opposite route but mass market distributors usually prefer sparkling wit to overt crudity. Restrictions on cursing need not be inhibiting; indeed, they can be liberating, forcing a subtitler to explore humor in the target language, as in this episode of *Cheers* ("Don't Paint Your Chickens", 1989), directed by James Burrows with a screenplay by David Isaacs and Ken Levine:

DR. FRASIER CRANE

> Congratulate the doctor. I'm doing a piece on the psychological ramifications of Ingmar Bergman's later works for *American Film*.

NORM

Oh, that's great Frase.

FRASIER

I'd like to read it to you to see if it's still accessible to the layman. . . . Now, I call the piece, 'Ingmar Bergman: Poet of the Subconscious.' The films of Ingmar Bergman...

NORM

Boy, who could forget her in *Casablanca*, huh?

FRASIER

No, no, you're thinking of Ingrid Bergman, I'm talking about Ingmar Bergman.

WOODY

Ingmar Bergman, the boxer?

CLIFF

No Woody, you're thinking of Ingemar Johansson.

SAM

You mean the guy that knocked out Floyd Patterson?

NORM

No, no, no, Sonny Liston knocked out Patterson.

PETE

Who knocked out Johansson?

NORM

Patterson.

STEVE

Before Liston?

NORM

No, Johansson knocked out Liston.

CLIFF

Well, who knocked out Patterson?

WOODY

Was it Ingrid Bergman?

PETE

Ingrid Bergman...

FRASIER

[*yells*] Shut up, shut up! Not one more word. I came in here to discuss Ingmar Bergman, not to start an Abbott and Costello routine.

NORM

Actually, I thought it was more like Martin and Lewis.

SAM

You mean, Joe Louis?

CLIFF

Oh, he's the one who knocked out Floyd Patterson.

WOODY

Then who knocked out Lou Costello?

FRASIER

[*exasperated*] Apparently Ingrid Bergman.

WOODY

Boy, she was tougher than she looked.

Study, Study, Study

American films of the 1930s, '40s and '50s were subject to a certain amount of censorship. The Motion Picture Production Code was a self-imposed standard designed to monitor the film industry. Known as the Hays Code after founder Will H. Hays, it was adopted in 1930 by the Motion Pictures Producers and Distributors Association (MPPDA)—later the Motion Picture Association of America (MPAA)—and by 1934 had grown to full power. It was disbanded in 1968 when distributors adopted the MPAA film rating system. During the days of the Hays Code, films retained wit and double entendre but managed to do so without the shock tactics of lesser films. This gave the movies long life. "William Powell is to dialogue as Fred Astaire is to dance," wrote Roger Ebert in a review of *The Thin Man*. "His delivery is so droll and insinuating, so knowing and innocent at the same time, that it hardly matters what he's saying." Hollywood films from this period are gold mines of wordplay. Some dialogue skates dangerously close to vulgar, but never crosses the line, as in Howard Hawks' *The Big Sleep* (1946), based on the Raymond Chandler novel with a screenplay by William Faulkner, Leigh Brackett and Jules Furthman:

The Big Sleep (1946)

BACALL

Speaking of horses, I like to play them myself. But I like to see them workout a little first, see if they're front runners or come from behind, find out what their whole card is, what makes them run.

BOGART

Find out mine?

BACALL

I think so.

BOGART

Go ahead.

BACALL

I'd say you don't like to be rated. You like to get out in front, open up a lead, take a little breather in the backstretch, and then come home free.

BOGART

You don't like to be rated yourself.

BACALL

I haven't met anyone yet that can do it. Any suggestions?

BOGART

Well, I can't tell till I've seen you over a distance of ground. You've got a touch of class, but I don't know how far you can go.

BACALL

A lot depends on who's in the saddle.

Subtitlers must learn the art of writing what's almost said. The dialogue in these films is surprisingly fresh even by modern standards. Any subtitle professional will find them useful primers for wickedly clever language acceptable to general audiences. Other American comedies worth studying: *Bringing Up Baby, The Lady Eve, The Thin Man, Trouble in Paradise,* and the Bing Crosby/Bob Hope road series. These films are invaluable references for translators working in television. Consider *The New Republic* film critic Otis Ferguson's comment on Bing Crosby's unique style of speech in a review of *The Road to Zanzibar*:

I believe him to be the first artist in popular expression today—not just slang for its own newness or to be different, but the kind of speech that is a kind of folk poetry, with its words of concision, edge, and cocky elegance fitted to speech rhythms, so that they may run free to the point, musical and easy.

The best translations have this sense of folk poetry. Exclamations and insults that were acceptable in the original country may be offensive to US viewers unless translated with the target audience's sensibilities in mind. Many exports to the US market represent the best of a country's films by screenwriters who know their way around wordplay. Put it in the subtitles.

Insults

Not all programs are witty company. Serious dramas also have much that can vex a translator. It's not easy to express the demeaning tone of certain inflections, verbs and phrases, but English has its own ways to insult. Subtitles can often replace the former with the latter. In Episode 51 of *East of Eden*, Shin Tae-hwan calls Dong-chul a dog and Dong-chul responds by calling Shin a rat:

TAE-HWAN

Look, it's the little doggy that keeps getting in our way. Tonight the mutt's dressed up as the president of Daehwa Construction. Lee Doggy-chul. You love spouting off about how bad I am but you're worse. You've always wanted to replace Guk Dae-hwa, and now the lil doggy finally gets his wish. Now the mutt's lifelong dream is coming true, nipping at the heels of the great Shin Tae-hwan himself.

DONG-CHUL

You've got the last part right. My whole life I've wanted to ruin Taesung and destroy you. Chairman Shin, I'm sure you've heard about rats. How they sniff out disaster and are the first to desert a sinking ship. Is it true? Does the rat have a feeling about the fall of Taesung?

TAE-HWAN

You really ARE Guk's doggy. Fearless, just like him. But how solid is a foundation built on dirty money? Let's just wait and see who falls first.

This translation uses the word "doggy" only slightly more than the original script, a choice that honors Shin Tae-hwan's veiled threats and insulting speech patterns. The invidious nuances in the dialogue are difficult to communicate in English. Dong-chul's response about the rat is literal and sounds right in light of this baiting tone. Shin Tae-hwan is an immature villain: he boasts while he insults. "Nipping at the heels of the great Shin Tae-hwan himself," the subtitles read, rather than the literal translation, "Trying to destroy Shin Tae-hwan." The phrase works with the doggy motif and communicates Shin's sense of self-importance. Dong-chul's response is mature and thoughtful. This variation retains the antagonism of the scene without resorting to crude name-calling.

Religion in Television and Family Films

American television audiences have come to expect a uniform blandness when dealing with religion. It's not that religion doesn't exist—quite the opposite. All religions exist and all are treated equally. The rule seems to be that religious *differences* do not exist. Mainstream television in the US leans toward a banality in presentation of religious beliefs. Consider the character Rose in *Lost*: she so completely inhabits her Christian faith that it doesn't seem remarkable when she invites another character to join her in prayer. The screenplay is character-driven, focusing on Rose rather than religion—and so creates natural dialogue in the bizarre world of the program. It is safest to adopt the inoffensive phrasing preferred by US networks when translating a family film or television program for mass market distribution. Just as distributors err on the safe side, the translators they hire may wisely do the same.

Rating Systems

Buyers have shown a preference for televisions with controls that limit access to programs with specific ratings. Be aware of international ratings and their equivalents in America. This ensures the content of the subtitles is appropriate to the target market—the goal of any distributor interested in staying in business. Use exclamations suited to viewer expectations.

Chapter Five

Tone

The history of the different civilizations is the history of their translations. Each civilization, as each soul, is different, unique. Translation is our way to face this otherness of the universe and history.

—Octavio Paz

The subtitler's role is interpretive. Viewers may not know the language at all—or only a little—and are hoping for a sense of the original: its humor and pathos, tragedy and charm, romance and thrills. The subtitles must be transparent. Their tone must serve the original. Yet in this act of service a translator may create something truly worthwhile: a new version of the film that has never been experienced before. Consider opera soprano Renée Fleming's comment on interpreting a role as it applies to the source of a translation:

> In truth, it's the importance of the music itself, and of the work of the composer, that is the creative gift, while the role of the singer is relegated to that of *l'umile ancella*, the humble handmaid. From that perspective, singers are not artists themselves but merely interpreters of art. A few, however, can transcend craft and the efficient employment of a natural skill by honing that skill to the highest level.

Even when immersed in the original, subtitlers cannot escape their own perceptions and stylistic eccentricities. Audiences bring their own foibles and preconceptions to the experience, making each film unique for every viewer—indeed, for the same viewer multiple times. William James' famous observation on human perception is as true with film as any other human endeavor:

Enough has now been said to prove the general law of perception, which is this: that *whilst part of what we perceive comes through our senses from the object before us, another part* (and it may be the larger part) *always comes out of our own mind.*

Subtitles are not strictly solitary nor are they truly collaborative. They are interpretations of how one person represented the dialogue at a given moment. The translator as writer is forced outside well-trod paths onto new ground. Subtitles allow audiences to do the same.

The Spoken Word

Subtitles and written poetry are very similar. Poems are meant to be read aloud. Subtitles replicate spoken dialogue. Both deal with rhythm, cadence and inflection. Both are subject to space and time constraints. Leo Braudy writes:

> The defense of subtitles ideally stands for a belief in the primary need to preserve the integrity of the actor's projected personality, even at the expense of distracting somewhat from the purity of the visual image.

In Ingmar Bergman's *The Seventh Seal* (1957) medieval knight Antonius Block finds peace in a meal shared with a young couple and their child:

> I shall remember this hour of peace: the strawberries, the bowl of milk, your faces in the dusk. . . . I shall remember our words, and shall bear this memory between my hands as carefully as a bowl of fresh milk. And this will be a sign, and a great content.

Bergman's film is concerned with the silence of God. It does not shy away from meaningful questions. The dialogue is laden with religious imagery. This scene deals with a couple named Joseph and Mary. They have a young child. It is a moment of personal redemption for the knight, who has witnessed horrors and faces his own mortality. A translation must have the same depth of feeling as the original. Compare these subtitles:

> I shall remember this moment: the silence, the twilight, the bowl of strawberries, the bowl of milk. Your faces in the evening light. . . . I shall try to remember our talk. I shall carry this memory carefully in my hands as if it were a bowl brimful of fresh milk. It will be a sign to me, and a great sufficiency.

The first translation is serviceable. It communicates the intent and fits in subtitles. But it lacks poetry. It fails to capture the resonance of the dialogue.

The Seventh Seal (1957)

The second translation also fits in the space and time available, but does so with phrasing appropriate to the context. It leaves the viewer moved by the simplicity of the knight's personal revelation. The subtitler in the second example identified the tone of the entire film: the squire remains sardonic, Death enigmatic, the knight introspective. In each character there is an undercurrent of poetry. Every line has a subtle lyricism, just as in the original. Literary translator Octavio Paz comments on rhythm and tonality in translation:

> Poetry is the marriage of the sensual or physical half of language with its ideal or mental half. Poetry is 'impossible' to translate because you have to reproduce the materiality of the signs, its physical properties. Here is where translation as an *art* begins: since you cannot use the same language of the original, you must find equivalents. The text is lost but this effect can be reproduced through other signs; with different means, but playing a similar role, you can produce similar results. I say *similar*, not *identical*. Translation is an art of analogy, the art of finding correspondences. An art of shadows and echoes. . . . The literal is not a translation. Even in prose. Only mathematics and logic can be translated in a literal sense. Real prose—fiction, history—has rhythms and many physical properties like poetry. When we translate it, we accomplish the same as we do with poems: transformations, metaphors...

Not every film is a Bergman, nor is every line of dialogue a poem. But most have an overall tone. Even if many screenwriters worked on the project, as with TV, the feel of a particular program often remains relatively constant. Programs in ratings trouble may make a huge shift in tone in an effort to attract viewers, but even then individual episodes have a consistent style.

Identify the Overall Tone

Translation discovers the tone of the original author and does everything possible to replicate it. The actor's delivery, the source language, the screenplay—all must find their way into subtitles. Rainer Schulte refers to "the inherent tonal quality underlying words as sound spaces." Schulte acknowledges the stylistic role of repetitive text. He then adds:

> Equally important are the repetitions of sounds. However, the repetitions of the sounds and sound combinations are not as easily perceptible to the reader. . . . Are the emotional reactions of certain vowels in the source language the same as in the receptor language?

In the last scene of *Queen Seondeok*, the heroine dreams that she visits her younger self. Although her reign name was Seondeok, she is known by her given name throughout the program, Deokman. The older and younger Deokmans are played by different actresses, so for this scene the script identifies the same person with separate names, Seondeok (older self) and Deokman (younger self). Seondeok hugs Deokman on the street:

DEOKMAN

What're you..? Who are you? Listen, hands off! Listen, what's the idea, hugging people? Listen!

SEONDEOK

[*inner monologue*] Deokman, things will be hard for you. And very painful. You'll lose those that you love... and be so very lonely. It will be bleaker than the bleakest desert.

DEOKMAN

Wait, who ARE you? Why you crying?

SEONDEOK

[*inner monologue*] It will seem like you have everything. And yet, you will have nothing.

DEOKMAN

I swear... you're weird.

SEONDEOK

[*inner monologue*] And yet you must go on. You knew that, didn't you? [*speaking*] Go on. Forever on.

Observe the difference in tone and phrasing between the older and younger Deokmans. In the source, Seondeok's last two lines are actually the same verb, repeated with subtle variations. The English subtitle replicates the tonal quality of the original, repeating *go/fo*— and *on/on*. The verb used in the final line is often translated as "endure" or "survive", but both are forced and wrong in this scene. Young Deokman is just beginning her great adventure. She is full of hope. The older Seondeok is sad, yes, but also smiling, wistful. In the *Making of* special, writers Pak Sang-yeon and Kim Yeong-hyun discussed this point:

PAK

It's an understated message of hope. 'Go on.'

KIM

The ending is already so sad without adding the 'Forever on.' I'm worried how it will be received.

But the fact remains, there's a feeling of going on. The young Deokman, the old Deokman, all Deokmans everywhere. The message is the same. 'Go on. Forever on.' I don't think we need to overstate this sense of hope.

"And yet you must endure" has a sense of doom. "Survive" is even worse. "You must go on" means the same thing but implies a hopeful future, however bleak. If "go on" is a positive way to express the first sentiment, then "forever on" is a poignant way to replicate the subtle shift in verb endings. This translation honors the original's power and intent. It echoes the nostalgic tone of the dialogue and offers encouragement.

Tonal qualities occur in the cadence of born storytellers. Louis Armstrong often shared childhood tales with audiences, like this alligator anecdote from a Chicago performance in 1962:

> I was tellin' about the time when I was a little bitty boy in my mother's hometown of Boutte, Louisiana. I was about five years old, cute little ol' thing, too. Mayann, my mother you know, she said to me one morning, 'Son, run down to the pond and get a bucket of water for your mama.' And I cut out for that water, and Mayann dug me when I come back without the water and pooooh, boy! She said, 'Boy, where is that water?' I said, 'Well, mama, there's a big old rusty alligator in that pond and I didn't get that water.' 'Don't you know that alligator is as scared of you as you are of him?' I told her, 'Mama, if he's scared of me as I am of him, that water isn't fit to drink.'

Note the repetition of "little bitty boy" and "cute little ol' thing" and how Armstrong ends three consecutive breath points with the word "water". The story is rich with Armstrong's voice, told in his slow, deceptively-meandering style. But suppose Robin Williams told the same anecdote. It might flash by so fast the subtitles would have no time to register. It would need a heavy edit:

> I was a little bitty boy in Boutte, Louisiana. I was about five years old, cute little ol' thing. My mother, she said to me, 'Son, run down to the pond and get a bucket of water.' And I cut out for that water, and when I come back without it, poooh, boy! She said, 'Boy, where's that water?' I said, 'Well, mama, there's a big old rusty alligator in that pond.' 'Don't you know that alligator is as scared of you as you are of him?' 'Mama, if he's scared of me as I am of him, that water isn't fit to drink.'

Charlie Barnett, Tommy Dorsey, Benny Goodman,
Louis Armstrong and Lionel Hampton
A Song is Born (1948)

This shaves off 35 words. It retains Armstrong's speech indicators. Often a character's effusiveness gives dialogue charm. Editing even one word hurts. Keep as much as possible, but when the patter is coming fast, get to the point. Simplify. The sacrifice must be made to honor the pacing of the original and help viewers stay immersed in the program. As Ezra Pound observed in his translation of the 13th-century Italian poet, Guido Cavalcanti: "I have invented nothing, I have·given a verbal weight about equal to that of the original, and arrived at this equality by dropping a couple of syllables per line." Above all, subtitles must match the tone of the original.

Exploring the Source

Subtitles are multi-cultural and often interdisciplinary. A translator forever grapples with the source language: reaching, expanding, exploring referents and allusions. Each screenplay has numerous character voices as well as the unique tone of the writer. This is especially true with literary adaptations. From Emmy-winning screenwriter Larry Brody:

> The way I see it, the key to adapting literary material from any print medium is to be really familiar with the material. You have to know it backward and forward and sideways. It has to become part of you, as though it's your own original creation. The most important thing you can do is know exactly what effect the original has on the reader and understand why it has that effect. Normally you're adapting material because it's already proven itself to be successful. . . . Going to the heart and soul of the original and bringing them to your new medium is, I think, the key to successful adaptation.

Brody's advice on adapting screenplays is particularly relevant to subtitlers. Translation is adaptive—identifying the appeal of the source material and communicating it to the audience. Language and how it is used by the work's author changes with each new project. Translator Christopher Middleton calls this sense of newness and mystery in the source language "the other":

> It may be I translate as a compulsive pursuit of 'the other', which at times can take other forms. I don't mean this in a metaphysical way; but I do think that growth comes through encounters with the alien, the foreign, the strange, and the unknown. And one of the simplest and most creative ways of considering the act of translation is to regard it as a minimal, perhaps vestigial, but still exemplary encounter with 'the other'.

Subtitlers that reduce translation to moving words from one language to another fail to discover anything new. Their craft lacks art. Understanding a screenplay is an act of exploration.

History. In Episode 53 of *East of Eden*, the villain Shin Tae-hwan misquotes a Chinese classic, *The 36 Stratagems*. Worse, he attributes it to Sun Tzu's *Art of War*. *The 36 Stratagems* is often called *The Secret Art of War*. Knowing this, the screenwriters do a number on Shin Tae-hwan. The character is not stupid. It's likely that he knows that he's misquoting and giving the wrong attribution. He just doesn't care:

> 'Sowing Discord.' From *The Art of War*. A strategy that uses an enemy's allies to betray him. Given the right circumstances, any ally can turn traitor.

This misquotes the "Gaining Ground" section of *The 36 Stratagems*: Strategy 25—Replace a pillar with rotten wood. Rather than write "Gaining Ground" for this translation, the subtitles use a more straight-forward phrase, "Sowing Discord." This has the proper tone while honoring the intent of the dialogue—Shin Tae-hwan's rephrasing to suit his purpose. In Episode 54, Shin Tae-hwan again quotes the *The 36 Stratagems*:

SHIN

'Steal the ladder.' Bait your enemy onto the roof, then steal the ladder. It's a tactic from *The 36 Stratagems*.

HENCHMAN

Get him on the roof and *take* the ladder?

SHIN

Steal the ladder. After Lee Dong-chul is arrested for drugs what can Jacky bargain with?

HENCHMAN

So you'll...

SHIN

Play one against the other. Ruining Dong-chul isn't enough. I'll pull the ladder out from under Jacky, too.

Shin Tae-hwan is quoting Strategy 28: Coerce an enemy to a point of no return with ruses and false promises. His misquote is a matter of poor pronunciation. The subtitles have Shin Tae-hwan use the world "steal" and his henchman the word "take" to illustrate the subtle difference. The script clearly identifies the work referenced.

This scene plays on multiple levels. Shin's dialogue is shaded with a need to show-off. Viewers familiar with the classics will recognize Shin's mis-quotes and enjoy his preening arrogance all the more. Those unacquainted with the Chinese texts will still find the scene a wicked bit of villainy. The script plays with words, teases them, and in doing so, offers a rich verbal style that the subtitles must attempt to replicate. The tone is intentionally inconsistent. The translation must be inconsistent in the same way.

Mood. Each work has its own atmosphere, moods, tonal qualities, and repetitions of themes and phrases. Capturing the tone of a film requires understanding the original and something more, as noted by Edwin Honig:

> Translation discovers the text's other voice, its significant expressibility, not the mechanical transmissibility of content simply to serve the reader. . . . Many translations fail be-cause the translator is readily disabled by following a false notion of fidelity to the original instead of being faithful to his own total view of its imaginative import. . . . It is only where all is a transforming act fully engaging the imagina-tive faculty that the translation merges with the original.

Screenplays suffer greatly from poor subtitles, especially literal transla-tions that more often than not communicate something totally different from the spoken dialogue. The source has a unique tone. Poor subtitles fail to capture it, to share it with the viewer. Mood must be understood to find its way to the screen.

Puzzlers. No mysteries are quite like puzzlers. Fans of the genre enjoy their unique tone and pacing, from *The Da Vinci Code* to Indiana Jones, Scooby-Doo to Harry Potter. Puzzlers allow audiences to explore clues with the characters. Subtitles for word games should contain all the key terms of the riddles. They don't have to be expert puzzles, but they should follow the rules as established in the screenplay.

Episode 32 of *Queen Seondeok* features a magic square that reads the same horizontally and vertically. The camera zooms on the square. It is filled with Chinese characters that are as perplexing to the original audience as they are to US viewers. The hero reads the square and explains its meaning. The magic square terms—cryptic in both languages—are phrased with a tonal emphasis that warrants single quotation marks:

'Bright-sun-shine'... When the bright sun shines...
'Sun-shine-bright'... The sun will brighten the sky...
'Shine-bright-light'... and light will shine on all people.

This is a relatively simple word game. The subtitles create a structure that fits the magic square requirement and includes words used in the dialogue. The puzzle terms use equivalents that fit the overall context. This scene set the stage for an important magic square later in the episode, when a scholar inserts key phrases in a message to the king:

> Your unworthy servant fears that Silla is in danger of disappearing. The Royal house will fall. Look after our homeland.

The heroes solve the riddle by identifying hidden words. A literal translation fails completely to capture the tone of the scene:

DEOKMAN

'Silla is in danger of disappearing.'

YUSIN

The character '*so*' means disappearing.

DEOKMAN

'The Royal House will fall.'

YUSIN

The character '*yeop*' means to fall.

DEOKMAN

'Your unworthy servant fears...'

YUSIN

The character '*do*' means fear or concern.

DEOKMAN

'Look after our homeland.'

YUSIN

The character '*seong*' means looking closely.

DEOKMAN

'*So yeop do seong.*' Pronounced differently, it says '*soyupdo*'. Look at the *soyupdo*? [*grabs the soyupdo dagger*] What could be written there?

YUSIN

Calligraphy. Thin brush calligraphy.

Non-English terms cheat the viewers of their chance to solve the puzzle. These subtitles seem like a lesson in Chinese characters. Once Deokman picks up the dagger, the meaning of *soyupdo* is clear, but the scene is dull and plodding. The mood is lost. Better to adapt the original message and its explanation to an English-language word game structure:

LETTER

Your unworthy servant fears...
the Royal House may fall.
A dagger points at the heart of Silla.
Look after our homeland, I beg you.

DEOKMAN

'Your unworthy servant fears...'

YUSIN

Let's see... the first word is 'your'.

DEOKMAN

'The Royal House may fall.'

YUSIN

'Royal.'

DEOKMAN

'A dagger points at the heart of Silla.'

YUSIN

Next, 'dagger'.

DEOKMAN

'Look after our homeland, I beg you.'

YUSIN

'Look.'

DEOKMAN

'Your royal dagger look.' Rearrange the words and it makes sense. 'Look at your royal dagger.' [*grabs the dagger*] What's on the dagger?

YUSIN

Calligraphy. Thin brush calligraphy.

The audience can clearly see the riddle. Viewers discover the solution with the protagonists, honoring the intent and meaning of the scene. There are no cheats. The clues are there. Subtitles should be as playful and puzzling as the original.

Literary styles and allusions. Adapting the source's literary style is an essential part of subtitle translation. For example, metaphors tend to blend in many Korean novels, dependent on and inseparable from each other. But American audiences are accustomed to clear linear distinctions. These subtitles from a scene in *Damo* adapt a Western metaphorical style:

SE-UK

Your 'trail' only led to a cliff... and death.

SEONG-BAEK

Wrong. My bleached bones may crumble, but when I'm gone others will walk this path. In time their spirits will fill the valleys, their blood the rivers, until at last we forge a new road, a new world. Though I die... it is not... death.

This might be literally translated as, "In time their blood and spirits will fill the valleys and rivers," but a linear approach communicates the intent and vigor of the original in an easily recognizable style. The script alludes to a well-known Korean poem. The subtitles use a strident tone to echo the parallels with one of Korea's most famous *sijo* sonnets by Jeong Mongju (1337-1392). Jeong was passionately loyal to the old Koryo dynasty, which led to his assassination by the new Yi regime. The screenplay compares Jeong to Seong-baek—who supports old traditions in rebellion against the current Yi Dynasty. Seong-baek's dialogue echoes Jeong's poem:

Though I die and die again,
A hundred times dead,
Though my bleached bones crumble
And whether my soul exist or not,
This heart belongs to my lord—
How could it ever change?

Literary sources. The Captain Alatriste series by Arturo Pérez-Reverte displays how significantly tone can affect audience perception. The novels are told in the first person by Alatriste's protégé, Íñigo Balboa. During the course of their adventures, readers learn as much about Íñigo as Alatriste. Margaret Sayers Peden's translation of the opening paragraph in the first novel delivers necessary information while setting the tone for the series:

Alatriste (2006)

He was not the most honest or pious of men, but he was courageous. His name was Diego Alatriste y Tenorio, and he had fought in the ranks during the Flemish wars. When I met him he was barely making ends meet in Madrid, hiring himself out for four maravedís in employ of little glory, often as a swordsman for those who had neither the skill nor the daring to settle their own quarrels.

This dialogue was lifted from the novel in Agustín Díaz Yanes' film, *Alatriste* (2006). Compare Íñigo's voice-over in the final scene:

He was not the most honest man nor the most pious, but he was brave. His name was Diego Alatriste and he had fought with the infantry regiments in Flanders. When I met him, he was surviving in Madrid on unsavory tasks, often renting his sword for 4 maravedís to others who possessed neither his bravery nor his boldness.

The Fox Latina subtitles use only 59 words to the 74 in the book translation. Yet viewers get a clear image of how Íñigo sees Alatriste—brave and bold, a survivor. The subtitles honor the tone of the film and that of the source novel.

Know the referents. Many films are self-conscious. Consider Bill Bixby's famous line in *The Incredible Hulk* (1978): "Don't make me angry. You wouldn't like me when I'm angry." The clip aired at the beginning of each episode and is fondly remembered by fans. Thirty years later, screenwriter Zak Penn paid homage to Bixby in Louis Leterrier's *The Incredible Hulk* (2008). When confronted by angry thugs, Edward Norton's character stumbles over his poor Portuguese, delivered in subtitles: "Don't make me... hungry. You wouldn't like me when I'm hungry." Audiences laugh at the joke itself as well as the reference to a beloved program. As with *Inglourious Basterds*, the subtitle was written first and then translated into dialogue, but even then Penn had to be aware of the original line to make the gag work. Were this being translated, imagine how wrong the tone would be if the subtitler did not know the reference. This rule also applies to internal referents, as in Edwin Justus Mayer's screenplay for Ernst Lubitsch' *To Be or Not to Be* (1942). A Nazi collaborator is attempting to win the actress Maria over to his side and into his boudoir:

SILETSKY

In the theater it's important that you choose the right part.
In real life it's more important to choose the right side.

MARIA

I once played a spy. But I got shot in the last act.

The self-conscious reference to her dual role as an actress who *played* a spy and an actress asked to *be* a spy makes this scene work. Particularly in light of how the former ended.

Know the actor's persona. A subtitler must be aware of an actor's persona. Consider the power of Clint Eastwood's performance in *Unforgiven*. His screen image from previous roles gave great weight to the later film. This is true of Jean Gabin in *Touchez pas au grisbi*, Sean Connery in *The Russia House* and *The Untouchables*, Peter Falk in *Wings of Desire* and Marlon Brando in *Last Tango in Paris*. Viewers enjoy the film for the current performance and for those that went before. Some actors' on-screen personae are so carefully cultivated that their dialogue from film to film remains true to type. Humphrey Bogart contributed "Here's looking at you, kid" to the screenplay of *Casablanca*. He used "kid" ever after: twice in *Dead Reckoning* and again in *Tokyo Joe* and *Sirocco*. His 1951-52 radio show with Lauren Bacall, *Bold Venture*, is filled with dialogue indicators (including "kid") that came to be equated with Bogart's unmistakable style. He played against type in *The African Queen* while conveying the old wounds and buried nobility of his earlier roles. Communicating a screen personality's speech patterns in subtitles requires a deft touch. They must carry all the appeal of the original.

Chapter Six

Why Subtitles Matter

It will be a wonderful new art merging in a unified whole, presenting a synthesis of painting and drama, music and sculpture, architecture and dancing, landscape and man, visual image and uttered word. Recognition of this synthesis as an organic unity non-existent before is certainly the most important achievement in the history of aesthetics. This new art is the cinema.

—*Sergei Eisenstein*

Subtitles deal with what is seen and heard. They exist in tandem with dialogue, inseparable from the sounds and images on the screen. The trans-modal nature of subtitling offers translators unique opportunities for cooperation with the source program and its audience. Subtitles bridge a film's multiple semiotic modes by inserting word images that become part of a collaborative whole. Something new is created—a subtitled film. From Chuang Ying-ting:

> In the case of subtitle translation, semiotic modes, such as the spoken mode, the written mode, the mode of music, the mode of sound effects and the mode of moving images, become affordable with the aid of technology, and they operate in the subtitling process individually and collectively. As a result, to interpret the text of a film, or to be more specific, to decode the meanings of the text of a film, the subtitler has to deal with the meaning potentials generated from the multi-modality of the text.

Gunther Kress makes this same point: "In short, modes produce meaning in themselves and through their intersection or interaction with each other."

Few viewers that use English subtitles have mastery of the movie's original language. But they can see and hear and so may infer meaning from the film in much the same way language is learned. From Charles L. Barber:

> When we use the word *meaning* here, we are talking about the relationship between language and the real world, between the signaling system and the things that the signals refer to or stand for. We can call this *referential meaning*. We can only detect referential meaning by observing how language is used in actual situations, and this is how a child discovers the meaning of words and sentences when it learns its mother tongue.

Barber's referential meaning deals specifically with language acquisition but the lesson may be applied to the trans-modal nature of subtitles, where the written word is combined with the aural and visual signaling systems.

Criterion's 2008 release of Carl Theodor Dreyer's *Vampyr* (1932) illustrates how subtitles may integrate within a film to improve the whole. For years translating every word as spoken has been *de rigueur*. This is desirable for clarity. But with repetitive dialogue, equally repetitive subtitles fail to trust the audience, detracting from rather than enhancing the film. Translator John Gudelj and the Criterion staff provided subtitles that effortlessly blend with the dialogue. This artistry makes their unique choices even harder to spot.

Early in the story, protagonist Allan Gray stops in a country house. "Guten Abend," says the housekeeper. "Guten Abend," responds Gray. The maid's line is translated, "Good evening." There are no subtitles when Gray speaks. It would be pointless. The audience has heard this common banality and read the translation when first spoken. Nothing else is necessary. Later the heroine Gisele sees her sister Leone from the window:

There, outside. Leone, Leone!

The initial translation was necessary to communicate that the dialogue is actually a name, but when Gisele runs outside calling Leone's name, there are no subtitles. The lush imagery of Gisele running through the forest would be marred by a translation that hammers the obvious. When Gisele and Gray are fog-bound in their little boat, they yell, "Hallo!" and are guided by answering cries from the opposite bank. The context is absolutely clear without subtitles.

This technique was used to poignant effect when Leone rests in bed. "I am damned," she says. "Mein Gott, mein Gott... mein Gott." English-speaking audiences are familiar with the German phrase. Gudelj wisely translated the first lines, "My God, my God..." As the camera pans away from Leone, she whimpers the same line a third time. Here the subtitles are absent, allowing viewers to take in the full emotional impact of Dreyer's images.

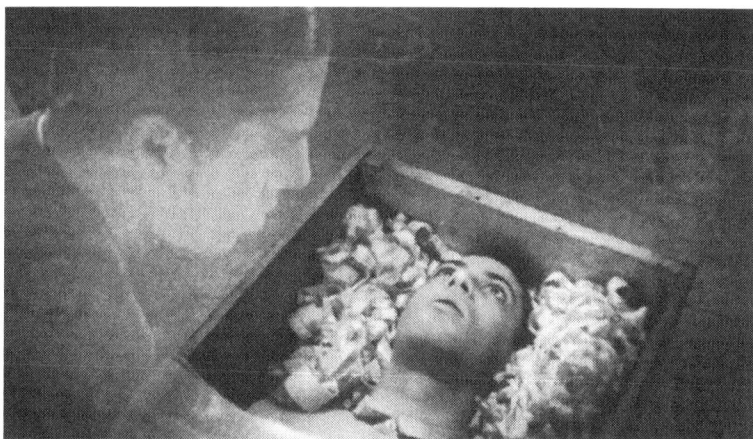

Vampyr (1932)

Collaboration between visual, aural and written modes requires a complete understanding of the source and target, as explained by Chuang Ying-ting:

> It is worth noting that, if one takes subtitling as a multi-modal practice, the source text is the film and the target text is the subtitled film. To be more specific, the subtitler has to consider the source or target text as a whole, rather than taking verbal modes as the major object to deal with and other visual and audio modes as merely the context. If the source or target text acts as a whole, the context should be the social and cultural environment in which the text is embedded, rather than other audio and visual modes. . . . Hence, the equivalence relationship between the source text and the target text in subtitle translation is very complex, because it does not deal with one-to-one modal translation, i.e., from dialogues into subtitles, but with multi-modal translation, i.e., from all the involved modes in the source text into all the involved modes in the target text.

Visual Cues

Word construction and film mechanics are quite similar, more so than the abstracts of painting, as Sergei Eisenstein explained:

> Now why should the cinema follow the forms of theater and painting rather than the methodology of language, which allows wholly new concepts of ideas to arise from the combination of two concrete denotations of two concrete objects? Language is much closer to film than painting is. For example, in painting the form arises from abstract elements of line and color, while in cinema the material concreteness of the image within the frame presents—as an element—the greatest difficulty in manipulation. So why not rather lean towards the system of language which is forced to use the same mechanics in inventing words and word-complexes?

Episode 33 of *Queen Seondeok* demonstrates how the similar methodologies of word and film construction can combine to make exciting visual entertainment. Yusin and Deokman are entered in a contest to discover the hidden meanings behind the name of their nation, Silla. The name itself is well-established in the program but the meanings are unknown to the audience and the protagonists. Solving the riddle on-screen requires explanations in dialogue. The original audience followed the investigation by *listening* as the characters spelled out their discoveries. A somewhat literal translation of the dialogue:

DEOKMAN

What's on the royal dagger?

YUSIN

Calligraphy. Thin brush calligraphy. '*Duk... up... il... shin. Mang... la... sa... bang.*'

DEOKMAN

Dukupilshin, Manglasabang?

YUSIN

- 'Mark each day with noble endeavors...

DEOKMAN

- ...bring the four corners unto yourself.'

YUSIN

That's it.

DEOKMAN

- Take the '*shin*' out of the first phrase...

YUSIN

- ...and the '*la*' out of the second.

DEOKMAN

That's the third meaning of Silla.

YUSIN

Dukupilshin, Mangrasabang. Together they spell Silla.

These subtitles are clear, but they hinder the flow and pacing of the scene. They read like a translation—a tedious one at that. This approach is known as *foreignization*, that is, retaining the film's cultural and linguistic features, bringing viewers to the source. *Naturalization* takes the source to the audience. It does not sheer away the foreignness of the original. Quite the opposite. It makes the foreign accessible. *Neutralization* promotes a neutering effect—removing local terms and cultural references from the subtitles and using explanatory notes when necessary. This is often used with dubbing projects and would make the *Queen Seondeok* scene almost nonsensical. Commercial subtitles usually take the naturalization approach, ensuring that the film is accessible while retaining the original's rich flavor. If this scene focused on a particular cultural aspect relevant to the plot, it should be included in the subtitles. However, the dialogue is part of the puzzle.

The Great Queen Seondeok (2009)

The subtitles must take these auditory clues and present them in a new medium, replicating the thrill of the chase in an entirely different mode. What would fail in dialogue may work in written form. In the following translation, the subtitles contain the necessary clues for viewers to follow how Deokman and Yusin solve the riddle:

DEOKMAN

What's on the royal dagger?

YUSIN

Calligraphy. Thin brush calligraphy. Solidarity... in ... Life. Longevity... for All.

DEOKMAN

Solidarity in Life and Longevity for All?

YUSIN

- Strength in unity...

DEOKMAN

- ...ensures survival.

YUSIN

That's it.

DEOKMAN

- Solidarity In Life... S-I-L.

YUSIN

– Longevity for All... L-A.

DEOKMAN

This is the third meaning of Silla.

YUSIN

'Solidarity in Life and Longevity for All.' The first letters spell S-I-L-L-A.

Viewers hear the actors' explanations, see the items discussed and read clues in the subtitles, combining a new written mode with the existing modes of the film. This requires a thorough understanding of each scene, its primary purpose, and how to include that in the new written medium. Gilbert C.F. Fong notes that subtitlers should make use of every semiotic mode available:

. . . in a subtitled film the written text does not operate by itself, but is accompanied and compensated for by other signs. And if the words do not fully convey the effect of the dialogue: for instance, its emotive value, they can be compensated by the tone, pitch and volume of the actor's voice, and by the actions, gestures and body movements, i.e., the body language. That is why some subtitlers tend to focus on information transfer and dispense with the dramatic quality of the dialogue, obviously thinking that it will be picked up by the audience during the course of the film. Needless to say, such an approach will usually result in the loss of colour and specificity. Subtitles are symbolic signs, and as such they should be fully utilized to contribute to the signification value. As they are already there at our disposal, it would be a waste to not put them to good use, to facilitate the communication process and to make the film-viewing experience more interesting and entertaining.

Visual Variants

It is an irony of subtitles that at their best they go unnoticed. They honor the original yet do not intrude on the experience of the film. Subtitles must never interfere. They should not read like a translation.

In Kim Kyeong-yong's *Someday* (2006), Kim Hee-jae's screenplay employs a charming bit of alliterative double entendre. A boy gets in a fight and earns himself a nosebleed. The heroine makes some coffee. By happy coincidence, the Korean pronunciation of coffee (*Copi*, like dopey) and the word for nosebleed (*kopi*) sound exactly the same. The heroine hands him a mug.

> Here's some *copi* for your *kopi*.

Coffee for a nosebleed? It makes no sense. But she can't resist her little wordplay. The phrase says much about the character—goofy, not at all self-conscious. "A little something for your nosebleed" communicates the meaning but has no alliteration or double entendre. It fails to show her playful side.

> Some yummy for your tummy.

This shares her alliterative phrasing but lacks double entendre. "Java for your lava" is too obscure. "Coffee for your owie" and "Espresso for your messo" are close. They're hokey enough—alliterative and at least the coffee-injury connection is there. The heroine is making a joke about coffee for the fighting nosebleeder. Spoken, the words *sound* the same. Read, they must *look* the same.

> Special of the Day. Macho Mocha.

The spoken repetition (*copi/kopi*) is represented in the written subtitles with words that trick the eye. They look similar. Gilbert C. F. Fong observed:

> Subtitles represent and re-present dialogue, which is speech, as writing; in this sense, subtitling is a cross-media transference of meaning and message: the process involves a double conversion, traversing from one language to another and from one medium to another.

"Macho Mocha" utilizes the new semiotic mode while retaining a sense of the playful, alliterative, corny dialogue. Such visual variants make subtitles part of the total viewing experience.

Word images can compliment a film. In Stephen Sommers' *The Mummy* (1999), the Egyptian dialogue scenes—and there are many—feature subtitles in a faux hieroglyphic font. Usually Arial is preferred: it is common, easy to read and inert. But Sommers was after a tone reminiscent of the Egypt of old Hollywood. Praising Karl Freund's original *The Mummy* (1932), Sommers wrote:

> For me, movies are at their best, and most fun, when they transport you to places or worlds that you've never seen before. Of course, *The Mummy* did just that, taking me to ancient Egypt in the 1920s and 1930s. It's those amazing Egyptian visuals that struck me as a kid and still get me even today.

Every aspect of Sommers' adventure horror film is informed by his enthusiasm for ancient Egypt. The unique subtitle font in *The Mummy* calls attention to itself, true, but very subtly. It is not merely utilitarian. It blends with the other semiotic modes to enrich the overall film.

Sommers' subtitles are equally innovative in *The Mummy Returns* (2001). The film ends at the Oasis of Ahm Shere. The villains are attacked by unseen forces. Their leader barks out a rapid series of orders in Egyptian. Normally there would be time for only one subtitle:

Fan out! Eyes open! Guns up!

But Sommers matched the subtitle to the actor's staccato delivery, similar to how computer print-outs or title cards unfold line by line, timed to be read by the audience. The first sentence appears; it remains on screen as the second sentence flashes next to it. Both are on screen as the last sentence joins them:

Screen 1: Fan out!
Screen 2: Fan out! Eyes open!
Screen 3: Fan out! Eyes open! Guns up!

Sommers effectively communicated the urgency of the scene in the time available, making the subtitles part of the scene itself.

The Mummy (1932)

Timur Bekmambetov's *Night Watch* (2004) takes visual variants to an extreme. The subtitles frequently dance across the screen in animated reflection of the dialogue itself. When a character yells, "Stop!!!" the words are in large font appearing all over the frame, similar to comic art, where a scream may be accented by bold, out-of-proportion text. A swimmer hears a voice. The subtitles appear near the character's head before dissolving into the water. Bekmambetov explained the unique contribution of subtitles to his thriller:

> We discussed with the studio how to make the movie more entertaining for English-speaking audiences. We thought of the subtitles as another character in the film, another way to tell the story. . . . Each time you confront another culture, it gives you the motivation to create something different, to rethink your film in a way.

Normal Non-fluency and Discourse Particles

Natural speech patterns are frequently referred to as normal non-fluency, that is, mistakes characteristic of ordinary conversation. Mick Short, an authority on stylistics, asserts that normal non-fluency is typified by fillers (*er, um*), pauses, mispronunciations, repetitions, grammatical structures that are abandoned, conversational turns that are lost, and competition between speakers to steer the conversation to a topic of their choosing.

> Normal non-fluency does not occur in drama dialogue, precisely because that dialogue is written (even though it is written to be spoken). Moreover, if features normally associated with normal non-fluency do occur, they are perceived by readers and the audience as having a *meaningful* function precisely because we know that the dramatist must have included them *on purpose*.

A 2009 re-release of Kim Ki-young's *The Housemaid* (*Hanyeo*; 1960) illustrates how removing a script's normal non-fluency from the subtitles can rob audiences of the vitality and pleasure of the original. Director Kim Ki-young knew his business as a screenwriter. The film's opening and closing sequences are often interpreted as bookends of reality enclosing a drawn-out fantasy tale. However, Kim is intentionally vague about 'fantasy' and 'reality'. The screenplay offers clues to Kim's intent. The subtitles should do the same.

The husband and wife begin the film speaking proper grammar. As the story progresses, the husband's decline and seduction is indicated by looser, stilted phrasing and expressions that echo those used by the uneducated maid. In juxtaposition, the wife's dialogue grows painfully correct. All of this is absent from the 2009 translation. Grammar is proper throughout, leaving audiences with a mistaken sense of erudition on the part of the children and the maid.

The husband's warmth—at times purposefully hackneyed—is entirely lost. In one scene, the wife mutters, "Having a young woman around the house is like offering a piece of raw meat to a tiger." The husband then turns to the audience and offers joking advice. Continuing the 2009 translation:

> How correctly you put it. Ladies and gentleman, as men get older, they spend more time thinking about young women. That's how they get drawn into women, which could lead to their destruction. This is true for all men.

South Korean melodramas during the 1950s and 1960s were targeted at a predominately middle-aged, married female audience, as observed by film scholar Kim Soyoung: "The melodramatic genre was considered an outlet for women to release their *han* (pent-up grief) over their experiences relating to repressive neo-Confucian patriarchy." The intense emotive quality of *The Housemaid* was designed specifically to appeal to these viewers, as was the director's skillful use of juxtaposition. Prior to this period in Korean film, breaking the fourth wall was primarily a comedic device. There are exceptions, but Kim Ki-young's viewers would have been familiar with this the kind of humorous interlude as seen in popular films and Korean folk performances. Kim uses this technique as catharsis to the melodrama preceding it and as bitterly ironic foreshadowing.

The tragedy that played out in the husband's mind informs his foolishly jocular speech to the audience. He seems doomed to fulfill his own fantasies. When he addresses the camera he steps out of the film and lets the viewers in on his little daydream. Men are men, he smirks. Compare this dialogue to the wife's invective earlier in the scene, the maid's wanton gasp of cigarette smoke and the subtle way the husband notices these facts. In this context the immediate segue into avuncular grinning dialogue takes on dark undertones. The husband's fantasy was fueled by awareness of this dynamic in the house. Later events may be informed by it. Consider this new translation that includes the wife's invidious dialogue and the boys' club humor of the husband:

WIFE

Having a pretty young thing in the house is no better than serving up raw meat to a beast.

HUSBAND

Meat? Beast? That's a fact. Ladies and gentlemen, as men age they find themselves thinking about younger women. That makes us easy prey and, well, everyone gets hurt. [*pointing*] You're no different... [*pointing another direction*] Oh, shaking your head? Uh-HUH!

The Housemaid (1960)

The first translation is not inaccurate. It is merely tepid. It captures the gist of the original but ignores the normal non-fluency of the dialogue and fails to match the action on the screen. The last subtitle line ("This is true for all men.") is almost nonsensical while watching the character. He is grinning, winking, pointing at audience members. His eyes glitter, his voice is jocular, his demeanor conspiratorial. This combination makes the source Korean film perfectly clear. ("You're no different... Oh, shaking your head? Uh-HUH.") The character's chatty tone should be included as accurately as possible within the time and space available.

The 2009 subtitles are also far too brief. They leave gaping holes between the spoken dialogue and the written word. The scene has plenty of time for the alliterative (meat/beast) and metaphoric (beast/prey) expressions of the husband's original speech. Kim Ki-young filled his film with dark comedy, pathos, wit and genuine emotion taken to grotesque extremes. All of this belongs in the subtitles. Jenny Mattsson's important study on the discourse particles (DPs) *well, you know, I mean,* and *like* in subtitling summarizes how small changes can have a big effect:

> Not all DPs can or should be translated in film subtitling. First of all, there is not enough space or time on either a cinema or TV screen to fit in translations of all DPs found in a film ST [Source Text]. Second, even if there were enough space and time on a screen, the excess of information caused by translating all DPs would in all likelihood wear out most film viewers, and interfere with other aspects of the film experience. Third, the polysemiotic whole of which the subtitles are part may include signals compensating for the loss of DP translations. Despite the fact that not all DPs can or should be subtitled, DPs in feature films are often included for a reason, and can be of importance for the characterisations of speakers, and for the overall interactional aspects of a film.

As Francois Truffaut said of Jacques Becker's *Touchez Pas au Grisbi* (1954), "He keeps only what is essential in the dialogue, even the *essential* part of the *superfluous.*"

Subtitle Relativism

Benjamin Lee Whorf's controversial hypothesis of linguistic determinism posits that language shapes thought. He asserted that different languages perceive and define reality in different ways. The Korean use of counter words to indicate the item being counted is an example of this. Whorf observed that the Hopi Indians have separate terms for water held in a container or in an open space; they also employ verb endings to indicate if a topic is an absolute fact, a memory, an expectation, a law, or a commonly-known truth. Eskimos have numerous words for snow, relevant to type. Whorf hypothesized that different languages necessitate different ways of thinking:

> We dissect nature along lines laid down by our native language. The categories and types that we isolate from the world of phenomena we do not find there because they stare every observer in the face; on the contrary, the world is presented in a kaleidoscope flux of impressions which has to be organized by our minds—and this means largely by the linguistic systems of our minds. We cut nature up, organize it into concepts, and ascribe significances as we do, largely because we are parties to an agreement to organize it in this way—an agreement that holds throughout our speech community and is codified in the patterns of our language. The agreement is, of course, an implicit and unstated one, BUT ITS TERMS ARE ABSOLUTELY OBLIGATORY; we cannot talk at all except by subscribing to the organization and classification of data which the agreement decrees. This fact is very significant for modern science, for it means that no individual is free to describe nature with absolute impartiality but is constrained to certain modes of interpretation even while he thinks himself most free.

"Strong" Whorfian linguists support this language-thought connection as deterministic; "weak" Whorfian scholars insist it is predispositive. A translator expands his world view, dipping into both languages for terms that identify elusive concepts, as explained by Kenji Hakuta: "One can stretch this weak Whorfian view a bit further and suggest that the bilingual is a happy thinker. Any given problem can be handled through two linguistic systems, and the languages can be alternated in search of the one that would more efficiently guide thinking." This puts subtitlers in a unique position.

Again from Whorf:

> The person most nearly free in such respects would be a linguist familiar with very many widely different linguistic systems. As yet no linguist is in any such position. We are thus introduced to a new principle of relativity, which holds that all observers are not led by the same physical evidence to the same picture of the universe, unless their linguistic backgrounds are similar, or can in some way be calibrated.

The subtitling apparatus is not a Whorfian calibration—indeed, nothing may ever be—but it is a challenging and intriguing approximation. Subtitles perform a synthesizing role. Translator and subtitler Corinne Imhauser:

> Just as the interpreter must take account of the speaker's body language as well as intonation and pauses when translating, subtitlers should therefore always bear in mind what appears on the screen and what is heard by the viewer. This should reduce the number of frequent mistakes made by translators who use the dialogue list as if it were a normal text and who do not always realise that visual or auditory clues may alter the meaning of the written dialogues. Such clues are also useful for dealing with polysemy or direct references to what can be seen on screen but is vague in the written transcription. In addition, relying on visual or auditory content will make condensation easier since part of the information normally available in a written translation can be either seen or heard by the viewer. Finally, the rhythm of the film/programme or of certain scenes is also meaningful and should be matched by the rhythm of the subtitles.

Translation is not for the timid. Subtitles add to existing semiotic modes to create a new experience. They bridge lexical gaps within and between divergent modes, affecting the film's perceived reality as a whole. Subtitles make it possible to peer dimly, imperfectly, into other patterns of thought.

Taking Responsibility

The subtitler's task can be a thankless one. Viewers may be unaware of the painstaking labor behind each line. But subtitling is part of a creative process that began with the screenwriter's first treatment. It affects international profits, as noted by Jacqueline Cohen, who subtitles Woody Allen films at LVT Laser Subtitling in France. Cohen told *TIME* correspondent Grant Rosenberg: "Whenever Woody comes to town, he always mentions that the reason his films are so successful in France is thanks to the person who does the subtitles."

Abé Mark Nornes takes this a step further:

> Filmmakers must involve themselves in translation because the contribution of the translator is every bit as profound as that of the screenwriter, actor, or director. . . . After all, in an age when no film is complete until it crosses the frontier of language, it is the translator who has the last word. Global cinema is the translator's cinema.

Commercial pressure to remove the translator's name and date of translation conveys a mistaken confidence—an implication that the subtitles were created as the film left the studio, part of the production process, approved by everyone involved. But translation is a separate activity, sometimes years removed from the theatrical release, rarely seen by the director. That fact should be explicit. There is a great deal of trust involved, as explained by Michael Cronin, Director of the Centre for Translation and Textual Studies at Dublin City University:

> Spectators of a film cannot judge the quality of the subtitles unless they speak the language and if the majority did, there would be no need for them. Their very existence assumes ignorance of non-native languages on the part of the spectator.

The presumed social contract between individuals in discourse is distinctly cooperative in cross-media translation. Subtitling is a mutual, though tacit, agreement with the audience. The subtitler navigates the linguistic terrain; viewers rely on their navigator for the best possible translation. "The placing of subtitles on the screen," writes Cronin, "gives a substantive reality to the existence of difference." A subtitler's name in the credits acknowledges this foreignness, takes responsibility and honors trust.

Taking Credit

In an industry where even caterers are listed in the end credits, translators' names are conspicuously absent. Caterers *should* be listed. They work hard and may hope to find future employment based on previous work. Subtitlers are no different, but home releases rarely list the subtitle team. Producers, editors and spotters commit time and considerable talent to the apparatus of subtitling. In a competitive industry, credit serves as promotion and reference. Proper acknowledgement is a business exigency.

The Joy of Discovery

Most subtitlers care about the words on the screen. Some keep at it work-a-day; others quickly burn out. Some continue as slaves to the text and give up hope that their effort will be recognized for the important part of global cinema it truly is. All are subject to editing and deadlines. All face harsh reductionism.

Yet they persist in this seemingly impossible task. "All translation is impossible and *that* is the reason why one does it," Michael Hamburger said. "I think all the things that are worth doing are impossible. Only impossible things are worth trying to do." It may seem absurd, but it is a wonderful absurdity, as eloquently expressed by translator Ben Belitt:

> That dilemma of absurdity! All translators knowingly participate in it, all openly confess it: it is one of the hazards of the occupation. . . . All translation is ludic, and not ethical. It turns into play the moment one moves out of the language of the original—the most serious play imaginable, since all knowledge hangs in the balance, or waits in the wings: the play with language, and possibility with utterance.

Subtitling is fun. It is thrilling to find just the right inflection, the perfect phrase that captures as much of the original as possible. Tone, style, double entendre, allusion, metaphor—a translation that communicates what is said and unsaid is a wonder to behold. It is a worthy endeavor. As Leo Braudy wrote:

> . . . movies at their best assert that art should transform individual life by making us into a new community through its power. Whatever their stories, whatever their methods, movies show us how to be human in ways that the other arts cannot.

Subtitlers accept the challenge to bridge cultural differences, to find common expressions and shared experiences that unite rather than divide. Viewers who know nothing of the source language can, through subtitles, come close to understanding it. The audience can share in the joy of discovery.

Every translator ought to regard himself as a broker in the great intellectual traffic of the world, and to consider it his business to promote the barter of the produce of the mind. For whatever people may say of the inadequacy of translation, it is, and must ever be, one of the most important and dignified occupations in the great commerce of the human race.

Johann Wolfgang von Goethe (1827)

References

Abbott, Bud and Lou Costello. *Who's on First: A Collection of Classic Routines.* On the Air (2000).

Akiyama, Nobuo and Carol. *Japanese Grammar.* Barron's (1991): 194.

Alatriste (2006). Directed by Agustín Díaz Yanes. Screenplay by Agustín Díaz Yanes from the novel by Arturo Pérez-Reverte. Subtitled by Fox Latina.

An, Ji-yoon. "Translators Are More Than Mediators." *Korea Herald* (09/26/09).

Barber, Charles. *The Story of Speech and Language.* Thomas Y. Crowell (1965): 231, 239, 263.

Beals, Jennifer. "*The Bride of Frankenstein*: In on the Mystery." Published in Milano, Roy. *Monsters: A Celebration of the Classics from Universal Studios.* Del Rey (2006): 87.

Berry, Wendell. *Collected Poems: 1957-1982.* North Point Press (1984): 258-9, 263.

Braudy, Leo. *The World in a Frame: What We See in Films.* University of Chicago (1976): 190, 233, 259.

Briggs, Anthony. "On Translating *War and Peace*.." Published in *War and Peace* by Leo Tolstoy. Penguin (2005): 1405. Translated by Anthony Briggs.

Brown, Ashley and John Kimmey. *Comedy: Modes of Literature Series.* Merrill (1968): 1, 3.

Buffy the Vampire Slayer. "Buffy vs. Dracula." (Season 5, Episode 1, 2000.)

—"Surprise." (Season 2, Episode 13, 1997.) Screenplays by Marti Noxon.

—*Buffy the Vampire Slayer: The Script Book Season Two Vol. 3.* Simon Pulse (2002), 1:32.

Bogdanovich, Peter. "Bogie in Excelsis." *Esquire* (September 1964).

Cameron, Deborah. *Feminism and Linguistic Theory.* MacMillan (London; 1985): 81-2.

Card, Orson Scott. *Characters & Viewpoint.* Writer's Digest Books (1988): 45.

The Cat and the Fiddle (1934). Directed by William K. Howard and Sam Wood. Based on the book by Otto A Harbach. Screenplay by Bella Spewack and Sam Spewack .

Charles, Ray. *Ray Charles: The Music That Matters To Him.* Hear Music (2002): 1.

Christie, Agatha. *Five Complete Hercule Poirot Novels: Death on the Nile.* Avenel (1980): 535.

Citizen Kane (1941). Directed by Orson Welles. Screenplay by Orson Welles and Herman J. Mankiewicz.

Cronin, Michael. *Translation Goes to the Movies.* Routledge (2009): 106, 115.

Cunningham, Ernest. *The Ultimate Bogart.* Renaissance Books (1999): 226.

Damo. MBC (2003). Directed by Lee Jae-gyu. Screenplay by Bang Hak-gi & Jeong Heyong-su. Excerpts translated by D. Bannon.

Dumas, Alexandre. *The Last Cavalier.* Pegasus (2007): 78. Translated by Lauren Yoder.

—*The Count of Monte Cristo.* Oxford University Press (1990): xxii-xxiii, 501. Reprinting the anonymous translation first published in 1846.

—*The Count of Monte Cristo.* Penguin (1996): 560, 1261. Translated by Robin Buss.

—*Œuvres Complètes: Le Comte de Monte-Cristo V. III, nouvelle èdition.* Calmann-Lévy (1889): 185.

Ebert, Roger. *The Great Movies*. Broadway Books (2005): 451.

Egoyan, Atom and Ian Balfour, ed. *Subtitles: on the foreignness of film*. MIT (2004): 30, 72-75, 85.

Eisenstein, Sergei. *Notes of a Film Director (Zamyetki Kinoryezhissyora)*. Dover (1970): 5, 85, 205. Translated by X. Danko.

—*Film Form: Essays in Film Theory*. (Harcourt, 1949): 60.

Falk, Peter. *Just One More Thing*. Caroll & Graff (2006): 140-41.

Ferguson, Otis and Robert Wilson (ed). *The Film Criticism of Otis Ferguson*. Temple University Press (1974): 356.

Fleming, Renée. *The Inner Voice: The Making of a Singer*. Penguin (2004): 156, 181.

Fong, Gilbert C. F., et al. *Dubbing and Subtitling in a World Context*. A collection of selected papers presented at the International Conference on Dubbing and Subtitling in a World Context, organized by the Department of Translation of The Chinese University of Hong Kong in October 2001. Gilbert C.F. Fong's paper was entitled, "Let the Words Do the Talking: The Nature and Art of Subtitling;' Chuang Ying-ting's paper, "Subtitling as a Multi-modal Translation;" and Corinne Imhauser's "The Pedagogy of Subtitling." The Chinese University Press (2010): 82-83, 91, 93-94, 101, 104, 232.

Frost, Robert. "Stopping by woods on a snowy evening." *The Poetry of Robert Frost 2nd Revised Edition*. Henry Holt and Co. (2002): 224-25.

Genet, Jean. *Prisoner of Love*. NYRB Classics (2003): 254. Translated by Barbara Bray.

Giddins, Gary. *Satchmo*. Da Capo Press (New York; 1998): 55.

Godzilla™ 2000 Millenium (Gojira ni-sen mireniamu). Toho (1999). Directed by Takao Okawara. Screenplay by Hiroshi Kashiwabara and Wataru Mimura. Dubbing script by Michael Schlesinger (TriStar; 2000). Godzilla is a trademark of Toho Co., Ltd. Subtitles courtesy Universe Laser & Video Co., Ltd., Hong Kong.

Goethe, Johann Wolfgang. *Goethe's Faust*. Anchor (1962): 145. Translated by Walter Kaufmann.

—Austin, Sarah. "Translator's Preface." Leopold Ranke. *The Popes of Rome: Their Ecclesiastical and Political History during the Sixteenth and Seventeenth Centuries Vol. 1*. John Murray (1847): vi. Translated from the German by Sarah Austin.

Grey, Zane. *West of the Pecos*. Walter J. Black (1931): 133-134.

Hakuta, Kenji. *Mirror of Language: The Debate on Bilingualism*. Basic Books (1986): 77.

A Hard Day's Night (1964). Directed by Richard Lester. Screenplay by Alun Owen.

Hammett, Dashiell. *The Novels of Dashiell Hammett*. Alfred A. Knopf (1965): 339-40, 436, 438-9.

Hecht, Ben. "Illustrations by Doré (Gustave)." Reprinted from Hecht's autobiography, *A Child of the Century*, in *West of the West: Imagining California*. Univ. of California (1989): 38.

Hemingway, Ernest. *Green Hills of Africa*. Scribner (1998): 22.

Honig, Edwin. *The Poet's Other Voice: Conversations on Literary Translation*. University of Massachusetts (1985): 7, 39, 73, 78, 155-59, 177-80, 201-3.

The Housemaid (Hanyo: 1960). Directed by Kim Ki-young. Blue Kino (2009). *The Housemaid Reference Book*. Translation Supervision: Professor Kim Eun Gi and June Oh with thanks to the Korea Literature Translation Institute. (2009): 38. New translation © 2010 D. Bannon.

Howard, Richard. Translator's Note to *The Little Prince* by Antoine de Saint-Exupéry. Harcourt (2000): x. Translated by Richard Howard.

Huston, John. *An Open Book*. Da Capo Press (1994): 409-10.

Jackson, Benson. *John Steinbeck, Writer: A Biography*. Penguin (1990): 835.

Jackson, Shirley. *The Haunting of Hill House*. Penguin (1984): 52-54, 85-87.

James, William. *Psychology*. Henry Holt (1892): 329.

Jensen, John. "Letters to the Editor." *The ATA Chronicle*, XXXVIII, 8: 11. Responding to a question regarding a statement made in his article "On Becoming a Literary Translator" as it appeared in the May 2009 issue of the same magazine: "We are often challenged to come up with such equivalences when nothing quite like the original will work."

Kim, Jonggil, ed. *Our Famous Poems (Uli-ui myeong si)*. Dong-A (1990): 262. Jeong Mongju's sijo translated by D. Bannon.

Kim, Soyoung. "Questions of Woman's Film: The Maid, Madame Freedom and Women." Published in McHugh, Kathleen, et al. *South Korean Golden Age Melodrama: Gender, Genre and National Cinema*. Wayne State University Press (2005): 190.

King, Stephen. *'salem's Lot: Illustrated Edition*. Doubleday (2005): 30.

—*The Stand: The Complete & Uncut Edition*. Doubleday (1990): 1017.

Koontz, Dean. *How to Write Best Selling Fiction*. Writer's Digest Books (1981).

Kress, Gunther, Carey Jewitt, Jon Ogborn and Charalampos Tsatsarelis. *Multimodal teaching and learning: the rhetorics of the science classroom*. Continuum (2001): 14.

Krevolin, Richard. *How to Adapt Anything into a Screenplay*. Wiley (2003): 194-96.

Kurosawa, Akira. *Something Like an Autobiography (Gama no Abura)*. Vintage Books (1983): 193-94. Translated by Audie E. Bock.

Lawrence, Jerome and Robert E. Lee. *Inherit the Wind*. Bantam (1960): 51.

Le Page, Robert Brock and Andrée Tabouret-Keller. *Acts of Identity: Creole-based approaches to language and ethnicity*. Cambridge University Press (1985): 181.

Lee, Yong-il & Choe Young-chol. *The History of Korean Cinema*. Jimoondang (1988): 120, 134. Translated by Richard Lynn Greever.

Leonard, Elmore. *Get Shorty*. Dell (1991): 3.

Let the Right One In (Låt den rätte komma in; 2008). Magnolia Home Entertainment (2009). Directed by Tomas Alfredson. Screenplay by John Ajvide Lindqvist based on his novel. Magnolia later released a version with both theatrical and home viewer subtitles.

Leyda, Jay. *Kino: A History of the Russian and Soviet Film*. Princeton University Press (1983): 410.

McBain, Ed (pseudonym of Evan Hunter). "I Saw Mommy Killing Santa Claus." *Ellery Queen Mystery Magazine* (January 2001): 88.

M'Crie, Thomas. "Provincial Letters XVI. December 4, 1656." *The Provincial Letters of Blaise Pascal*. Chatto & Windus (London; 1898): 305.

Mamet, David. *On Directing Film*. Penguin (1992): 76.

Mattsson, Jenny. *The Subtitling of Discourse Particles: A corpus-based study of well, you know, I mean, and like, and their Swedish translations in ten American films*. University of Gothenburg (2009): 267.

Milano, Roy. *Monsters: A Celebration of the Classics from Universal Studios*. Del Rey (2006): 87, 106.

Ming, Dong Gu. "Is Pound a Translator of Chinese Poetry?" *Translation Review*, 75: 54.

The Mummy (1999). Written and directed by Stephen Sommers.

The Mummy Returns (2001). Written and directed by Stephen Sommers.

National Union of Journalists. *Non-Sexist Code of Practice for Book Publishing*. London (1982): 6.

Night Watch (Nochnoy dozor; 2004). Fox Searchlight. Directed by Timur Bekmambetov. Screenplay by Bekmambetov and Laeta Kalogridis from a novel by Sergei Lukyanenko.

The No. 1 Ladies' Detective Agency. "Pilot Episode." HBO (2008). Directed by Anthony Minghella. Screenplay by Richard Curtis and Minghella. Based on the novels by Alexander Mccall Smith.

Nornes, Abé Mark. *Cinema Babel: Translating Global Cinema*. University of Minnesota (2007) 242-3.

Oppenheimer, Judy. *Private Demons: The Life of Shirley Jackson*. G.P. Putnam's Sons (1988): 211.

Pérez-Reverte, Arturo. *Captain Alatriste*. Putman (2005): 1. Translated by Margaret Sayers Peden.

Pileggi, Nicholas. *Wiseguy: Life in a Mafia Family*. Simon & Schuster (1986).

Pound, Ezra. "Guido's Relations." *The Translation Studies Reader, 2nd Edition*, ed. Lawrence Venuti (London: Routledge, 2004): 92.

Puzo, Mario. *The Godfather*. NAL Trade (2005): 28.

Rizzo, Alessandra. "Luciano Pavarotti Obituary." *The Boston Globe*. Sept 6 2007.

Rosenberg, Grant. "Rethinking the Art of Subtitles." *TIME*. May 15, 2007.

Rostand, Edmund. *Cyrano de Bergerac: A Play in Five Acts.* R.H. Russell (New York; 1898): 293-94. Translated by Gladys Thomas and Mary F. Guillemard.

—*Cyrano de Bergerac.* Penguin Classics (2006): xv-xviii, 186-7. Translated by Carol Clark.

—*Cyrano de Bergerac.* Oxford French Series. Oxford University Presss (1921): 306.

Schickel, Richard with Jeffrey Ressner. "Travolta Fever." *TIME Magazine.* October 16, 1995; Volume 146, No. 16.

Schulte, Rainer. "How Should a Translator Walk through a Text?" *Translation Review,* 75: 1-2.

Scott, Helen and Francois Truffaut. *Hitchcock/Truffaut: Revised Edition.* Simon & Schuster (1985): 139.

The Seven Samurai (Shichinin no samurai; 1954). Criterion Collection (2006). AK 100: 25 Films of Akira Kurosawa (2009). Written by Kurosawa Akira, Shinobu Hashimoto and Hideo Oguni.

The Seventh Seal (Det sjunde inseglet; 1957). Criterion Collection (2009). Written and directed by Ingmar Bergman.

Shertzer, Margaret. *The Elements of Grammar.* Collier Books (1986): 142.

Short, Mick. *Exploring the Language of Poems, Plays and Prose.* Addison Wesley (1996): 176-177.

Simon, Neil. *The Sunshine Boys.* Samuel French (1973): 13-14.

Someday. OCN (2006). Directed by Kim Kyeong-yong. Screenplay by Kim Hee-jae. Excerpt translated by D. Bannon.

Sommers, Stephen. "*The Mummy*: Adventure Reborn." Published in Milano, Roy. *Monsters: A Celebration of the Classics from Universal Studios.* Del Rey (2006): 106.

Sudley. Introduction to *The Three Musketeers* by Alexandre Dumas. Penguin Classics (1952): 24.

Stegner, Wallace. *On Teaching and Writing Fiction.* Penguin (2002): 79-80, 90-91.

Strunk, William and E. B. White. *The Elements of Style, Fourth Edition.* Longman (2000): 7.

Sullivan, Clare. "On Translating Badly: Sacrificing Authenticity of Language in the Interest of Story and Character." *Translation Review,* 75: 13, 18.

Tarantino, Quentin. *Inglourious Basterds: A Screenplay.* Weinstein Books (2009): 6, 19-20, 26, 43.

Touchez pas au grisbi (1954). Criterion Collection (2005). Directed by Jacques Becker. Based on Albert Simonin's novel. Screenplay by Becker, Simonin, and Maurice Griffe.

Trouble in Paradise (1932). Directed by Ernst Lubitsch. Screenplay by Grover Jones and Samson Raphaelson from a play by Aladar Laszlo.

Trudgill, Peter. *On Dialect: social and geographical perspectives.* Oxford (1982): 164-5.

Truffaut, Francois. *The Films in My Life (Films de ma vie).* Simon & Schuster (1978): 179. Translated by Leonard Mayhew.

Turk, Edward Baron. *Hollywood Diva: A Biography of Jeanette MacDonald.* Univ. of California Press (1998): 135, 194.

Twain, Mark (pseudonym of Samuel Clemens). "How to Tell a Story" and *The Adventures of Huckleberry Finn.* Reprinted in *The Norton Anthology of American Literature, Shorter 4th Ed.* W.W. Norton (1995): 1202, 1281, 1387-88.

Vampyr (1932). Directed by Carl Theodor Dreyer. Criterion Collection (2008). *The Vampyr Reference Booklet.* German with English subtitle translation by John Gudelj. (2008): 43.

Wall, Brian and Michael Zryd. "Vampire Dialectics: Knowledge, Institutions and Labour." *Reading the Vampire Slayer,* ed. Roz Kaveney (Tauris: London, 2002): 60.

Webber, Elizabeth and Mike Feinsilber. *Dictionary of Allusions.* Merriam-Webster (1999): 221.

Weiss, Ken and Ed Goodgold. *To Be Continued....* Bonanza (1972): viii.

Whedon, Joss. *Firefly: The Official Companion: Vol. Two.* Titan (London: 2007): 9.

Whorf, Benjamin Lee. *Language, Thought and Reality: Selected Writings of Benjamin Lee Whorf.* John B. Carroll, ed. MIT Press (1956): 114, 213-214.

Wright, Kate. *Screenwriting is Storytelling: Creating an A-List Screenplay that Sells!* Perigee (2004): 178, 196.

Printed in Great Britain
by Amazon